Clearing Clutter

as a

Sacred Act

Essays, Poems, and Practices

Written and Illustrated by

Carolyn Koehnline

Gentle Approach Publications
Bellingham, Washington

Gentle Approach Publications
Bellingham, Washington
United States of America

ISBN: 978-1-7329543-0-4

All illustrations, including the cover art, are by Carolyn Koehnline, except for the photograph on page 122, contributed by a friend, and the photo of the author on page 154, taken by Lifetouch®.

Cover design by Marc Hoffman (www.SongbirdPhoto.com)

The purpose of this book is to educate, inform, and enlighten those persons who wish to use the exercises and essays for self-knowledge and personal growth. It is not meant to replace psychological or medical treatment.

Carolyn Koehnline can be contacted through
www.GentleApproachCoaching.com

Acknowledgments

Much gratitude to my friend and mentor, journal therapy pioneer Kathleen Adams. Through her teachings and her visionary organizations—The Center for Journal Therapy and the Therapeutic Writing Institute—I've learned crucial tools that have infused all my work.

Many thanks to my dear friend and accountability partner Kim Scanlon, who first suggested I be a clutter consultant back when I was in graduate school studying psychology and cleaning houses for a living. Her deep listening and original perspectives continue to bless my endeavors.

I will be forever indebted to my dear friend and mentor, Helene Block, who taught me my thoughts were worth listening to, and who, after all these years, is still listening.

I am grateful to my beloved Dominique Coulet du Gard for her steadfast support and vital input.

Much gratitude to Marc Hoffman, who has steadily believed in me and supported me technically and artistically throughout the years.

And many thanks to my parents, Bill and Phyllis Koehnline, for encouraging my art, writing, and unconventional approach to life, while showing me work can be meaningful and satisfying.

I also wish to thank:

Tina Blade for her exquisite editing.

Marline Lesh for her careful reading and suggestions.

Susan Smith-Pierce for her supportive brainstorming.

The students and clients who have allowed me to work with them and have been my teachers in the process.

Mary Reynolds Thompson, Kate Thompson, and Clare Cooper Marcus for deepening my understanding of the relationship between people and spaces.

My morning journal group: Laura Shelton, Kathie Hardy, Claudia Ackerman, and Joan Wildfield for their willingness to humor me no matter what I invited them to try, and for adding their brilliance to my work.

My coach, Lianne Raymond, who has gently helped me find my own way to marry practical progress with sacred intention.

The cedar tree I visited regularly throughout the process of writing this book.

My journal, in all the forms it has taken throughout the years, for helping me access wisdom, compassion, and clarity.

All the help, seen and unseen, known and unknown.

This book is dedicated to my mother

Rev. Phyllis G. Koehnline

Table of Contents

A Sacred Approach

C learing *Clutter as a Sacred Act* grew out of my twenty-five years as a psychotherapist, clutter coach, trainer, journal keeper, and journal therapist. This book is also informed by my own struggles and experiments as a human being on this planet, and how I've found ways to access the support I've needed, inside and out, to navigate my life.

Life is messy and challenging. It doesn't fit into tidy packages. And it's constantly changing. So if you have some clutter, it's not evidence that you're broken or unworthy.

If you've identified some clutter that it's time to clear, it's also not surprising if you've been avoiding it. Many of us do. Clearing clutter can present some unexpected challenges.

This book addresses the mixed emotions we often feel toward those things we're looking to give up, as well as the fear and excitement that can arise when we're creating space for something different or new. Approaching this challenge in a sacred way honors the depth and complexity of the task.

Before we get started, I want to define some terms that you'll encounter frequently throughout this book. In fact, I'll let the words *Clutter, Transition,* and *Sacred* define and introduce themselves.

CLUTTER

"I am a metaphor. I'm also solid and real. I show up in homes, heads, hearts, and schedules. I am the problem that sends you in search of help. I evoke humility because I represent so concretely the choices you've made, the experiences you've had, what you've done, and what you haven't done. You might get overwhelmed when you look at me. I'm seen as a door-blocker and an embarrassment behind the scenes. But there's more to me than that. I hold clues to what needs a goodbye and what is still waiting to happen. I'm mixed in with treasures. Even though people tend to avoid me, they often find that, when they turn toward me, good things can happen. I'm often more willing to be released than people suspect."

TRANSITION

"I'm a reminder that clearing clutter is a process that can take you to someplace new. I make sense of messiness, discomfort, and goodbyes. I know that feeling lost and stuck are just part of a bigger unfolding. I'm about spring coming after winter and new beginnings coming out of endings."

SACRED

"I am a stance that respects the whole mix of who you are and the choices you've made. I connect you with endless hidden sources of energy and inspiration. I'm not about judging *whether you're worthy. I'm interested in how simple rituals and intention can help make this endeavor more meaningful and more possible."*

Many people don't experience clutter clearing as a sacred act. Often the process is accompanied by harsh words and cruel self-judgment, pressure, and panic. But when you begin that way, it usually leads to unfortunate decisions and bigger messes than you started with.

I offer this book in the hopes that it will steer you away from the negative, self-defeating aspects of clutter clearing and lead you toward the clarity, self-acceptance, and lightness that the process can provide when it is treated as sacred.

As you engage with this book and take stock of what you've accumulated, you'll be encouraged to weave intentional gestures of love and devotion into the process. You'll be exposed to techniques that can help you tap into inner and outer sources of courage and guidance, so you don't feel so alone.

You'll see how, at times, it can be important to approach clutter clearing with preparation and intention. Other times, it helps to do it on the fly, inserting it into the flow of your life.

Whenever you engage in clearing your clutter as a sacred act, it's a chance to make peace with your own imperfections and with life's ambiguities. It is an opportunity to decide what deserves your time, space, attention, and other resources. It is also an opportunity to strengthen your ability to face life's changes and to practice the essential art of letting go.

Tips on Navigating This Book

There are many ways to travel through this book. You might work through it chronologically from beginning to end, engaging fully in each suggested action. You can also open it to any page, read a poem or essay, or try out a writing process. You might use the book as a daily meditation, an occasional inspiration when you feel stuck, or as a constant companion. It's also quite possible—and totally fine—to start and restart the book several times before taking it on fully. If you lose it for a while in your clutter, it's possible it will reappear when you're ready to dive in deeper. This book and its underlying philosophy are all about helping you discover and apply the approaches that work best for you.

With that in mind, here are some tips for reading and engaging with *Clearing Clutter as a Sacred Act*:

- ✧ As you read my words and write your own, notice what intrigues you.

- ✧ Notice anything that brings a feeling of lightness where there's been heaviness.

- ✧ Notice what brings clarity where there's been confusion.

- ✧ Use this book any way you like to help get some movement where you've been stuck.

- ✧ This book has a companion website with worksheets, recorded entrance meditations for writing processes, and other resources designed to support your clutter-clearing process with gentleness, imagination, and sacred intention. To access those resources, go to:

www.ClearingClutterAsASacredAct.com/

No matter how you engage with this book, I encourage you to hold your own unique clutter-clearing process as sacred.

CHAPTER ONE

Making It Sacred

Making Room for the Muse

We need not be afraid.
A thousand gifts will flood the void when we
loosen our grip
and let our hands fall open.

Too easily we fill our minds, our hearts, our homes, with
frantic chanting on TV, crowding
jumbo cans from warehouse stores onto
shelves squeezed tight and flustered.

But if we open up our rooms,
inside-out,
make some space between the
nagging items on our lists,
there she will be,
our essential
though elaborate friend, reminding us that
if we look beneath the ugly road, a
true, tangled meadow will reveal itself,
stem by stem,
bloom by bloom.

Then will come the goddesses who
whisper music, dream honey,
play a delicate shadow symphony, leaving us
moon drunk to fiddle in our sleep,
dancers leaping round and round.

The tasks are important.
Our chores,
responsibilities,
keep our world in place.
Still, if we open up some space to
walk into our lives, buck naked,
love immensely what will leave us,
a thousand gifts will flood the void.

A thousand gifts will flood the void.

Dedicating Your Process

The clutter-clearing process is a look at reality. It shows you what you have and haven't done. It reveals evidence that some happy times are now in the past and some of your stories didn't turn out the way you wanted them to.

Many begin the process feeling enormous pressure to make rapid changes, as if scaring or bullying themselves into action might bring positive results. Although this approach can work in the short-term, it often fizzles over time. When we feel attacked, even by ourselves, we get defensive. We rebel, go shopping, or get unfocused and confused. We get lost mindlessly surfing the internet or go to the refrigerator even though we're not hungry. We go into fight-or-flight mode, or we freeze.

The sacred approach to clearing clutter, on the other hand, assumes the best in you. It is not about shaming or fixing you. Rather, it assumes that you are doing your best with what life brings you, even if that falls woefully short of your expectations. It does not expect or demand perfection. It simply invites you to make the process sacred in whatever way suits you.

You can start by dedicating this endeavor to something bigger than yourself. If it's just about being neater and tidier, you will quickly lose interest. Instead, let it be an offering to something deeper and more resonant for you.

For instance, what if you declared your process an act of devotion? An act of love? What if you dedicated it to something or someone that deeply inspires you?

✧ *This is for my children, who deserve plenty of space for their own lives.*

✧ *This is for Buddha, who practiced non-attachment.*

✧ *This is for Jesus, who preached love and forgiveness.*

✧ *This is for Mother Earth, who understands the process of letting go so new life can grow.*

✧ *This is for my muse, who requires space to share her gifts.*

✧ *This is for Kwan Yin, the goddess of self-compassion.*

✧ *This is for God, the source of all that I need.*

✧ *Once you've determined the recipient of your dedication, you might want to write a brief statement to deepen your commitment.*

I hereby proclaim that my clutter-clearing process is an act of devotion to my muse—the one who brings me creative inspirations. As I clear my clutter, I am making space for a deeper, more vibrant engagement with her, opening myself to new possibilities, and trusting that as I let go, richer treasures will come into my life.

Possible Actions

> ➢ Make a list of possible people, spiritual beings, ideals, and visions you could imagine dedicating your process to. Circle the one that feels most right.

> ➢ Write a brief statement of dedication and sign it. Then decide where you'll put the statement.

Creating a Sacred Container

Creating order can be messy. Simplifying can be complicated. When you turn your attention toward the clutter you've accumulated, you may discover pockets of chaos you hadn't even thought to worry about. What's more, major clutter clearing is a multifaceted endeavor that takes sustained effort. It can be helpful to have one place—like a folder, book, or box— to gather and hold your clutter-clearing process materials.

It doesn't have to be fancy. You can use a three-ring binder divided into sections, an open file box, or a digital folder on your computer with files for each category. Whatever you choose, it should let you easily sort and access information and writings related to the various aspects of your process. If another kind of container occurs to you, and it fits that criteria, that's probably the right choice for you.

If creating a container feels overwhelming, just skip this step for now. It may not be the right timing for you to create such a container. You can always choose to come back to it later.

If you do feel drawn to the idea of having one gathering place for your clutter-clearing process materials, here are some possible categories that could be represented by notebook sections or digital files:

INSPIRATIONS—Include quotes, poems, song lyrics, fortunes from cookies, images, scriptures, or pieces of your own writing that raise your energy and help you feel supported. It can be helpful to read them before your clutter sessions or when your energy and enthusiasm are flagging. You might also use this section as a place to list other kinds of inspiration— music to listen to or a walk to take.

RESOURCES—Include house cleaners, shredding services, professional organizers, haulers, thrift stores, upcoming community garage sales, websites, and other useful supports for your process.

PROJECTS—This is where you can track on different cluttered areas or categories of clutter. It can include worksheets, spreadsheets, plans, notes about where you left off, and before and after photos.

QUESTIONS—Questions will come up as you go through this process. Some will be research questions about where you can donate or sell an item. Some will be more emotional. It's helpful to have a place to park these questions so that even if you can't deal with them immediately, you'll be able to come back to them when you're ready. Writing questions down also gives them a place to "simmer on the backburner." When you return to them, you may have more clarity about your next step.

PROCESS WRITING—Most of the chapters in this book suggest writing processes to help you further explore, personalize, and make use of the perspectives and information being shared. You might want to keep all your writings in a "Process Writing" section of your container. You can also choose to write and keep them in a separate journal.

GOODBYES—This is a space for photos or writings related to significant or emotionally-loaded items you're releasing.

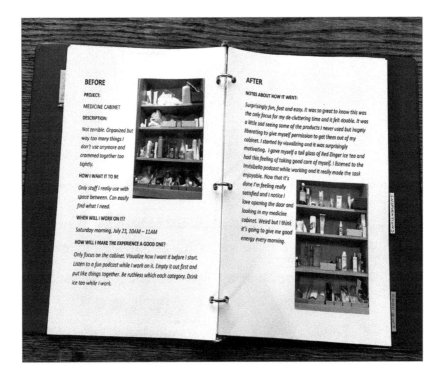

Don't worry too much about what sections to include. That will likely come clear to you with time. Just start with whatever makes sense for now.

Any system you create will be more useful to you if you find it engaging. Once you've decided on a container—whatever form it takes—think about how you can infuse it with sacred energy. Doing so will make it more alive for you. For instance, you might decorate it or write a special blessing for it.

May this Sacred Container hold with love and kindness the whole mix of what I'm facing. May the overwhelming feelings and chaos I bring to it be transformed into doable actions infused with meaning and hope. May the questions I bring find helpful answers. May it hold the big picture, even as it allows me to work on one thing at a time.

Possible Actions

➢ Imagine what kind of container would be a good fit for you. Describe it in writing or draw a picture of it.

➢ Create a quick and simple container or spend some time making it beautiful and inspiring.

➢ Think about how you could infuse your Sacred Container with the energy you are dedicating your process to. Decorate it, write a blessing for it, or find some other way that fits with your beliefs and sensibilities.

Naming Your Process

A woman I know was having a terrible time getting herself to weed her garden. The more the weeds took over, the more she avoided dealing with it. Whenever the word "weeding" showed up on her list of things to do, it just made her want to get in her car and go somewhere else.

The same thing can happen when you see the words "Clear the clutter," on your list of things to do.

One day the woman with the weeds woke up with an inspiration. "I'm just going to focus on revealing the beauty in my garden." She found this approach so motivating that she kept at her weeding for hours and got the whole garden done.

"Revealing the Beauty" could be an inspiring title for your clutter-clearing process. Here are some more possibilities:

- *My Transformation Ritual*
- *Making Room for Adventures*
- *Creating Space for Peace*
- *Claiming My Space*
- *Claiming My Life*
- *Making Room for Love*

Possible Action

> ➤ Spend five minutes brainstorming a list of possible titles to inspire your process. Circle the one you like best.

CHAPTER TWO

A Trustworthy Companion

The Ideal Helper

Dealing with clutter can be lonely. It can feel like everyone else is having fun or doing important things while you're stuck mucking around with piles of stuff from your past. You might also find that, left to your own devices, you don't make much progress.

Maybe you don't want to take on this task alone. But maybe you're also too embarrassed or afraid to ask for help. You might be worried that if you let someone into your process, they would shame you or pressure you to get rid of stuff you want to keep.

Clutter is vulnerable territory. But getting help when you need it can be vital to your process.

If you could dream up the perfect support, what kind of clutter-clearing companion would be most helpful to you? Picture and describe them.

> *My ideal helper is a gentle older woman, like my grandmother—100% non-judgmental. She showers me with love and completely believes in me. She trusts that I'll find my own way. When I'm confused, she lets me talk about it. She notices when I need a break and has iced tea and snacks ready when I need refueling. When she's there, I believe in myself.*

My ideal helper is a big strong guy who can move anything that needs moving. He has a great sense of humor and gets me laughing when I start to feel bogged down. He puts on upbeat music that keeps the energy flowing. He's playful and teases some, but he doesn't go too far. He always comes up with great ideas when I feel stuck. He also shares his goofiness and imperfections with me without shame. He helps me feel like I'm just fine and I can do this.

My ideal helper is rigorous and no-nonsense but kind, like my fourth-grade teacher. She has a clear plan for us to follow, and she keeps me from getting lost in distractions and daydreaming. She has a big chart on the wall and crosses off items as we accomplish them. She nudges me to decide things when I want to avoid them. She motivates me to do my best.

Possible Actions

> ➤ Make a list of qualities you'd want in your ideal helper.

> ➤ Write a description of your ideal helper as if she, he or it was a character in a book. You might want to sit quietly for a few minutes or draw a picture before beginning to write. Or you might choose to listen to a recorded entrance meditation to guide you into writing about your ideal helper at:

> www.ClearingClutterAsASacredAct.com/

> ➤ After you've written for five minutes or so describing your ideal helper, read what you've written aloud. Then write a sentence or two about anything that emerges as helpful or important from this process.

Finding Helpful Help

Once you have a sense of the qualities you're looking for in a helper, think about the people you know who have those qualities. Is there someone you could trade time with, hire, or accept help from as a gift?

You might know someone who is willing to help for free. That's wonderful—unless it's not. Be judicious about who you pick to be your clutter helper. Sometimes people who would be generous with clutter-clearing time and energy are not the ones to allow into your messiest spaces. Don't invite someone who is overly fond of bossing you around and feeling superior. Watch out for people who are just looking for free stuff.

I also encourage you to be careful about bringing onto your team those who are genuinely supportive but lack the necessary skills. For instance, if they are distracting and scattered, they can unintentionally derail your progress and leave you with more of a mess.

Before you let someone into your home to help you, make sure they have enough of the qualities and skills you're looking for. They don't need to be perfect. But don't feel you must say yes to people who haven't earned your trust. Also, be clear about whether they are offering their help as a gift or expect payment. Ask them questions and check in with yourself to assess whether they're likely to be respectful and genuinely supportive of you.

Sometimes people choose a spouse, partner, or housemate to help them. This sometimes works beautifully. It can certainly be convenient. But if the people who live with you feel frustrated or resentful about the way your belongings have intruded on their space, they probably won't be your best helpers. There's too much emotional clutter in the way. It's best to choose someone who isn't personally invested in what you keep and what you release.

Once you've found a helper who seems like a good fit, it's still up to you to give them guidance about how they can be most helpful. What kinds of instructions would you want to give them? Here are some examples:

> ✧ *Just go through this area and put like things together so I can go through them and decide what to keep and what to let go of.*

> ✧ *I'll be making all the decisions, but it would really help if you'd haul away and deliver the things I'm discarding and donating.*

> ✧ *I'd like you to just hold up each piece of clothing and ask me, "Do you really, really love it?"*

> ✧ *When I get stuck, please help me puzzle through my decisions out loud.*

> ✧ *Please just bring over your own project to work on. You don't really need to help me at all. Just be a kind presence so I don't feel so alone.*

> ✧ *You don't need to be with me in person. But can I send you brief emails or texts to report on little victories? If*

you respond with congratulations on my progress that would be extra helpful.

Possible Actions

> ➤ Brainstorm a list of possible helpers from the people you know or have heard about.

> ➤ Spend five minutes writing instructions you would want to give a helper, so they would be truly helpful to you. Allow yourself to write down whatever occurs to you and see what comes of it. You can always revisit and revise your instructions later as you get more clarity.

Consulting Your Journal

Sometimes you won't want anyone intruding on your process. Maybe you feel too unfocused or vulnerable. Or you can't find or afford to hire the ideal person. Whether or not you have someone helping you, your journal can provide a different kind of help.

A journal is simply a blank book that invites you to write in it. It can be fancy, bound leather with a beautiful cover; a cheap spiral notebook; or anything in-between. It can be paper or digital. The important thing is that it's a trustworthy companion. Onto your journal you can intentionally project the wisest, kindest, most patient and loving person or being you can imagine. This will be who you're talking to when you write in it.

When your journal holds the energy of a trustworthy companion, it frees you to write in it honestly. This can change how you listen to your own thoughts as they spill onto the page. It can help move you past self-judgmental yammering and allow you to discover more productive, compelling territory. It makes room for the whole mix of hopes and fears, clarity and confusion. That kind of spaciousness can bring fresh insights and open the way for self-compassion.

There are many ways your journal can be helpful to you in this process. Here are a few:

✦ *DO SUGGESTED WRITINGS.* At the end of each essay in this book, you'll find brief, focused writing processes to help you personalize and apply the information you've just read. You might choose to write in your journal or in a section of your Sacred Container—the clutter notebook, box, or dedicated computer folder you've chosen to hold your clutter-clearing process materials.

✧ *ASK A QUESTION.* If you're stuck and can't figure out what to do next, you can reach for your journal, ask it a question, and then write for five minutes. Do this even if you doubt it can help. Each time I try this, I notice that at the end of the writing I'm in a different frame of mind than when I began. Chances are good that will happen for you as well. You can ask practical questions like, *"What should I do next?"* or, *"What categories should I use for my sorting process?"* It's also good for questions that have an emotional component, like, *"Why am I having such a hard time deciding what to do with Grandmother's doll collection?"*

✧ *INVITE SELF-COMPASSION.* If you start asking self-critical questions, like, *"What's wrong with me?"* you can use your journal to turn that around and ask the question in a loving way. Ask as if you are talking to a dear friend who is struggling. *"What's wrong?"* Then your heart will be more open to sharing with you emotionally. You may discover some useful information about what's blocking you. What's more, this gives you the opportunity to express some thoughts and emotions that need expressing. That allows movement inside and out.

With this kind of process writing, you can skip long explanations. Your journal already knows the backstory. You also don't have to be brilliant, interesting, or a great writer. This is your private space. The key here is that, when you let the writing flow and take you where it will, wisdom can bubble up, sometimes in unexpected ways.

Letter writing is another technique I'll be inviting you to try in this book. Once I wrote my journal an apologetic letter in order to reconnect with it when I felt I'd been neglecting it. I got this response:

Dear Carrie—

Here's the thing you can always count on: You never ever have to worry about hurting my feelings. I'm just not built that way. You can ignore me, rip out my pages, even shred me, and I will be cheering for you if it helps you in your process.

My security is not dependent on any behavior from you. I am connected to a bigger source—the source where all journals and tools of healing get their power. So, do as you will. All is well. Naming me, decorating me, writing in me is good if it's good for you. If it's a distraction from what you need to do, forget it. Let it go. I am the one you can come to without having to worry about my needs. That is why I am such a powerful help to you. Any guilt you feel is self-imposed. For you, I have no agenda, only faith, love, and goodwill.

With that in mind, I invite you to write in peace.

Your Journal

May your journal be an equally loving and supportive friend.

Possible Actions

> ➤ Decide what kind of journal you want to use. Determine whether it should be its own separate book or included as a section of your Sacred Container.

> ➤ On the first page of your journal, take about five minutes to write a letter to it requesting the kind of help and qualities you're asking of it. Read the letter aloud, imagining that your journal is listening. Then write a letter from your journal to you and read that letter aloud. Make a note of anything that strikes you as interesting from this exchange.

> ➤ You may want to decorate the journal or find some other way to make it feel like it's yours.

When You Feel Incompetent

Faced with this challenge that seems so daunting
you may find yourself shrinking—
forgetting all that you know,
all you can do.

This is a time for breath,
stillness,
and kind, encouraging words.

Allow yourself to be a beginner with
the openness of a child for whom
everything is mysterious and new.
Let curiosity rule the day.

If you practice patience with your clumsiness and inefficiencies,
seek truly helpful help,
and allow yourself to be uplifted by those who believe in you
and those who have successfully traveled this path,

space will open for you to puzzle it out yourself,
settle into your own knowing,
and find your own way.

CHAPTER THREE

Casting Sheepishness
to the Wind

This Is Clutter

This can be sung to the tune of "My Favorite Things," ©1959 Richard Rogers and Oscar Hammerstein II.

Papers I've piled up for ages and ages.
Books I won't read. Some are missing some pages.
Puzzles with pieces I never will find.
These are some cluttering things on my mind.

All of the yeses I should have said no to.
All of the messes I still have to go through.
Tools for the hobbies I never will try.
These are some things that are making me sigh.

This is clutter. I don't need it.
I can set it free.
And when it is gone from my home, head, and heart
I'll finally have room for me.

Gifts I was given that I never wanted.
Memorabilia that makes me feel haunted.
Props for the life that's not me anymore.
Why I am keeping this, I am not sure.

All the excuses and all of the blaming.
All of the shoulds, and what-ifs, and the shaming.
All of the worries that get in my way.
Why not start clearing it all out today?

This is clutter. I don't need it.
I can set it free.
And when it is gone from my home, head, and heart,
I'll finally have room for me.

Summoning Your Courage

Clearing clutter is a courageous act. You may have already summoned that courage and feel ready to go. But if you find yourself avoiding, procrastinating, and getting distracted, it's very possible some fears are lurking.

That wouldn't be surprising. Clutter usually represents decisions and feelings we'd prefer to avoid. It can be helpful to list and name your fears to shine a light on them. Then they have less power over you.

Here are some of the possible fears that can arise when you're getting ready to clear your clutter:

- *I'm just going to make a bigger mess than I started with.*

- *I'm not capable of going through all this stuff. I'll get started, and then I'll stop. I'll just disappoint myself and everyone else.*

- *If I'm successful at clearing this clutter, I'll have to figure out what to do with the time, space, and energy the process has freed up.*

- *If I do this, people's expectations of me may increase.*

- *Going through this stuff is going to stir up emotions I can't deal with.*

- *All my past negligence and mistakes are going to be exposed, and I'll end up feeling like a real loser.*

- *If I start clearing clutter now, there's not going to be any time left for anything else. It's just going to go on forever.*

Fear can play a critical role in how we respond to change and the unknown. Growing up, I had fears about going to sleep without a light on, moving to a new house, riding a bike, learning to drive, and how I was going to make a real life in the adult world. Even though I managed to meet those challenges, I've still found lots to be afraid of as an adult.

I've learned to expect that there's a part of me that's going to look for reasons not to grow and change. It's trying to keep me safe. I've also learned that, unless I'm in mortal danger, I can't let that part of me be in the driver's seat. If I let it take charge, my life will be way too constricted.

If you're feeling brave and ready to dive in and confront the clutter in your living space, your schedule, and your life, go ahead and get started. But if you suspect that your fears could stop you, I encourage you to acknowledge those fears, then find a way to tap into a more courageous part of yourself. The following suggestions can help with that.

Possible Actions

➢ In your journal, name some of the fears that arise when you think about addressing your clutter. Add to the list any other fears you suspect may be lurking below the surface.

➤ Write the question, "What should I do with these fears?" Remember that when you write in your journal, you're consulting your wise, kind, patient companion. Spend five minutes writing, letting that wise companion answer your question. Don't stop to judge the answers. Just write whatever comes. You can decide afterwards if it feels right to follow through on any ideas that emerge from this exercise.

➤ Make a list of things you thought you couldn't do but were eventually able to do. Circle one, then write for five minutes about how you got past your doubts and fears.

➤ Write a description of someone you know or admire who is courageous. They can be real or fictional. Let yourself imagine that you are embodying their energy, and picture yourself confronting your clutter with ease and delight.

➤ Make a list of various props that could help evoke courage in you. What clothing could you wear? What hat or piece of jewelry could you put on? What could you listen to? What could you read? What blessing could you give yourself? What image could you look at? What aspect of nature could you summon to help you?

Adjusting Your Focus

When I first got a pair of bifocals, I was fascinated with how they allowed me to both look closer and see farther. I called them my "super-crone" bifocals. I had to train myself to use the bottom half of the lens when I wanted to read and the top part when I wanted to see at a distance. Otherwise, my eyes automatically found the line in between and everything looked blurry. I had to become very mindful about how I was focusing at any given moment. With time, my eyes adjusted, and this new way of focusing came more naturally to me.

The chaos of clutter creates its own kind of blur. The clutter-clearing process asks that we focus differently at different stages and develop the ability to shift from one view to another.

THE BIG PICTURE: It often helps to begin by getting a bird's eye view of the situation. This is not a time to notice and zero in on tiny details. Rather, it's a time for big-picture questions like:

✧ *What are the types of clutter I've accumulated?*

✧ *Which spaces are most cluttered?*

✧ *How big an endeavor will this decluttering process be?*

FOCUSING WITHIN: Where and how should you begin this process? You might find that there's an obvious, logical place to start and sequence of steps to take from there. If not, it may be more productive to turn your gaze inward to sense the feelings that surround the different areas and types of clutter. It often helps to start with an area or category of clutter that frustrates you on a regular basis and also feels emotionally possible to address.

ZOOMING IN: Once you've chosen a clutter-clearing project, it's time to look closer and put a frame around it.

✧ *I am just focusing on sorting my shirts.*

✧ *I'm only going to work from ten to noon.*

✧ *My focus for this session will be this one cupboard.*

Once you've defined your frame, it's time to put on blinders and screen out the various demands and distractions that may be vying for your time and attention. Give yourself permission to tune in to the details of your chosen area of focus.

CLOSED EYES: If you get lost in the minutia of a stack of papers, or they're all starting to look alike, give yourself a focus break. The brain can only take so much mindful focusing at a time. Maybe it's time for a nap, a walk, or some other soothing, non-focused activity.

LOOKING BACK AND LOOKING FORWARD: There are times in this process for noticing where you've been, what's happened, and the feelings your emotionally loaded objects from your past are still holding for you. You'll learn more about that in chapter seven. But there are other times when it's helpful to look forward—to envision the living space and the life you'd like to create.

You can learn how to imagine and explore those possibilities in chapters eight and nine.

SOFT EYES: If you start to get self-critical, it's time to soften your gaze, tune into your heart and breath, and reconnect with this endeavor as an act of devotion.

If you find yourself getting stuck, notice what kind of focusing you've been engaging in. See if it's time to shift your focus.

Possible Action

> ➤ Write for five minutes about your typical modes of focusing. Do you tend to focus mostly on the big picture? Do you often get stuck in minute details? Which ways of looking do you over-emphasize? Which ones do you under-emphasize? Read what you've written aloud. Then write a sentence or two about anything that strikes you as interesting or important.

Naming Your Clutter

As you approach the challenge of clearing clutter, it can be helpful to define the different kinds of clutter you want to clear. But it can also be stressful. As you read through the various types of clutter mentioned here, notice if you start to get overwhelmed. If so, I encourage you to breathe slowly and deeply. Put your hand on your heart and say something encouraging to yourself even if you don't fully believe it.

PHYSICAL CLUTTER includes the papers and objects that have piled up in one specific space or throughout your home. Maybe there's a certain type of object—boxes, shoes, building supplies—that have become an issue. There may be a category of things related to a past career, relationship, or loss. Maybe you've saved every piece of paper that looks even vaguely important or interesting. Maybe you have an unsorted mishmash of stuff, and you haven't a clue what's there. Whatever physical clutter you're addressing, it's likely that some other kinds of clutter are also in the mix.

DIGITAL CLUTTER includes the piled-up emails, outdated digital folders, multiple versions of programs, and extra stuff you don't need or understand, all clogging your computer and phone.

MENTAL CLUTTER can consist of overthinking, needless worrying, repetitive negative thoughts, scattered thoughts, and unresolved decisions. It is the excess baggage in your head that drains your energy, distracts you, and blocks your way.

EMOTIONAL CLUTTER includes the excess baggage that accumulates in your heart—resentments you're holding onto, fears you haven't faced, unexamined judgments, dreams you've pushed aside, and goodbyes you've avoided feeling or even acknowledging.

SCHEDULE CLUTTER eats your time. It includes yeses you should have said no to, time-wasting activities, being too available for everyone else, trying to do everything at once, misplaced perfectionism, and an absence of planning.

There are many ways these different categories of clutter can overlap and be interrelated. For instance, the objects and papers we stuff into boxes often represent decisions we don't want to make and feelings we don't want to feel. Cluttered schedules can be a sign of confusion about what's important to us. A cluttered space can create mental fogginess and depress our energy.

As you name and figure out the kinds of clutter you'll be addressing, you're taking a courageous step. You are mapping out the territory. It's important to be kind to yourself during this stage; remember you don't have to deal with everything at once. You'll be practicing ways to break the job down and make it doable.

For now, you're just in a process of naming. Doing so will help bring your various kinds of clutter out of the darkness and into the light so you can address them more effectively.

Possible Actions

> ➤ Walk around the space you plan to work on and make a list of cluttered areas it feels important to address. Look for areas that aren't functioning well, seem neglected, drain your energy, or don't feel intentional. Don't address them. Just list them. Keep breathing as you do this. If self-criticism arises, say something kind and encouraging to yourself, like, *"I'm proud of myself for looking at this." "I'll get to each thing in its own time." "My self-worth is not dependent on my being perfect."*

> ➤ Make a list of some categories of clutter that seem ripe for the clutter-clearing process. You don't have to know for sure that you'll be getting rid of them. Just trust your intuition about what kinds of objects need a fresh look to determine whether you love them, whether you need them, and whether they resonate with who you are today.

> ➤ Look over both lists and circle any items you feel some readiness to address. Remember that it probably doesn't make sense to start with the most difficult, complicated, emotionally loaded areas or categories of clutter. Finish by writing a few sentences about anything you figured out in this process.

Your Relationship with Your Clutter

There is a relationship going on between you and your clutter. It might be clinging, estranged, hostile, or sentimental. It's possible that it's based on a confusing mix of emotions and assumptions.

Once you've begun to name the kinds of clutter you'll be confronting, consider writing a letter to your clutter. That might seem strange. But doing so can help you begin to identify and give expression to any feelings you are holding about it. As you write, just let your true feelings flow. Notice the tone you take as you address your clutter. You may or may not be surprised by what emerges.

You can write to clutter in general, like this:

Dear Clutter,

That's it. I'm so sick of you. You have got to go. I've had it. No more making me feel guilty. No more talking me into reasons for keeping you...

Dear Clutter,

I hate to break it to you, but it's time for us to part. I am so appreciative of all the gifts you gave me...

Or you can write different letters to specific kinds of clutter:

Dear Inherited-from-My-Aunt-Minnie Clutter...

Dear Ceramic Dog Collection...

Dear Don't-Want-to-Admit-I-Made-a-Mistake Clutter...

Possible Actions

> ➤ Make a list of the kinds of clutter you could imagine writing a letter to. Circle the one that intrigues you the most. Then spend five minutes writing the letter. Try not to overthink it or control what comes out. Remember that doing this kind of practice is a leap of faith and an act of devotion, even if it seems a bit weird or silly. Be willing to be surprised by what you write. When you're done, read it aloud, imagining that your clutter is reading the letter and hearing your words.

➢ Write a letter of response from your clutter to you. Start with Dear (your name). Again, be willing to be surprised by what comes out of your pen or shows up on your screen as you tap away at the keyboard.

➢ After reading the response, write down a sentence or two about the current relationship between you and your clutter. What does it tell you about the stance you want to take from here on out? Can it be gentle and encouraging? Do you need to set firm boundaries? Will you need to approach the process of clearing the clutter as more of a transformation ritual or more of a battle? Write your sense of what will help the process go well.

Your Relationship with Your Home

How are you feeling about your home these days? Apologetic? Hopeless? Proud? Lucky? Disappointed? Do you judge your home? Do you feel it judging you? Are members of your household battling for coveted spaces? Does your home feel too small? Do you love it or just make do with it?

Clearing your clutter is sometimes about making yourself at home in your living space, whether that space is a tiny house, a farmhouse, a suburban home, a trailer, or a city apartment. This can be challenging. There are all kinds of reasons people find it hard to feel "at home."

If you struggle with this, maybe you never learned to fully inhabit a space. Some people just never unpack. Maybe you left behind a home you loved, and you can't get used to the new one. Maybe when you look around your home, all you can see are things that need to be fixed, changed, decluttered, or cleaned up.

Feeling disappointed in your home, unworthy of it, or as though there's no space in it for you, will affect your willingness to engage with it. To make your clutter-clearing project successful, it's helpful to establish a relationship with your home that is as warm and kind as possible.

Exchanging letters with your home can be a helpful way to open the lines of communication with it. Even neglected, chaotic, or troublesome homes are often surprisingly generous spirits, very willing to welcome you, assist you, and share useful information with you.

If you can't get used to a new home because you're grieving for a past one, you might write a letter to say goodbye and to express appreciation to the home you left behind. Doing so can free up energy for a fresh relationship with the new place.

If you can't figure out what to do with a particular room, you might ask for its opinion. The room might have thoughts about how it could be arranged, what's most important to repair and what can wait, and how you might change its décor.

If a home truly isn't a good fit for you or your family, that might become blatantly obvious in the letter-writing process.

Whether you feel that you're communicating with the spirit of your home or connecting with a part of your brain you don't normally access, the process can be enlightening.

Possible Actions

> Write a letter to your home, just saying whatever comes to you. Be truthful about your thoughts and feelings. Write for five minutes—or longer if you feel so inclined.

> Read the letter out loud. Then write a response from your home starting with Dear (your name). Read that letter aloud. When you've completed the exercise, write a sentence or two reflecting on any insights or information that emerged from this process.

In Praise of Imperfection

There is no one perfect thing to do.
So there. I said it. Shame on you
little voice inside
for even trying to fool me.
Yes. I know you're lying
when you try to say that there's a way
to make a perfect minute, day,
vacation, marriage, whole life story,
pure perfection in its glory,
never itchy, never dopey,
never scratchy, never pokey.
I plan to give all that a rest.
From you, I'm making this request.
Let me practice. Let me bungle.
Let me muddle through this jungle
of unfinished this and forgotten that
and things I've swept under the mat.
Without your judging and your nagging
My inspiration won't be flagging.
I'll get it done imperfectly.
Only that will set me free.

CHAPTER FOUR

A Gentle Plan

Set Your Course with Kindness

Some clutter-clearing and organizing books have a precisely defined and specific recipe for making change. You move from A to B to C in a straight line to get to the goal of an orderly and clutter-free home.

Luckily, for those of us who have a more meandering style, there are other ways to reach a destination. A sailboat is a useful image for me in this regard. Sailboats never travel in straight lines. But good sailors don't let themselves be blown about randomly all over the water. They sight something to steer towards, then pay attention to everything around them—the weather, the wind, and the tide—to make their way to their destination. They listen to wisdom from those people they trust, and they follow their own instincts and common sense to get where they want to go.

Clearing clutter can be like that. You need to work with fluctuations in your mood and energy, and with the changing circumstances of your life as you work to make progress. You often can't map it out exactly ahead of time. You probably won't move in a straight line. But in each clutter session, you might identify what you're steering towards. This helps you keep the bigger picture—your destination—in mind. It's also helpful to have some gentle instructions to guide you and some reliable ways of checking in with your inner wisdom along the way.

If you don't intentionally set your course, you will likely fall into old unhelpful habits. The following are some examples of self-defeating ways people approach clutter clearing because they haven't consciously and realistically set themselves up for success. Notice if any of these are familiar:

✧ Be vague about the goal.

✧ Don't put the session on your schedule.

✧ Approach the endeavor with a combination of enormous expectations and a total lack of confidence in your ability to make changes.

✧ Try to do everything at once.

✧ Don't take breaks.

✧ Sit, stand, or squat in an uncomfortable position, and set things up as inconveniently as possible.

✧ Pretend that you're not thirsty or hungry and work past the point of exhaustion.

✧ Focus on how much you haven't accomplished and how much more there is to do.

✧ Criticize yourself throughout the process.

✧ Set yourself up for frequent interruptions.

If you want to create a more successful clutter-clearing session, review the list above and do the opposite. You might also write out your plan, considering the details of the task with care and kindness. Here's an example of such a plan:

At ten o'clock Saturday morning, I'll work for two hours focusing on the stuff piled up on my desk. That's my only focus. I don't have to worry about the rest of my office or any other rooms in the house. I'll start by doing a quick sketch of my dream desk and what I'd want to have on it. It doesn't have to be perfect. I'm dedicating this session to my writing life. I'll have a cup of coffee in my favorite mug, just the way I like it. I'll also put on some instrumental jazz that energizes me without making me too hyper. Probably guitar. My hope is to remove and relocate anything that doesn't belong there and to be very intentional about what gets to live on my desk. My fear is that I'll get overwhelmed and bogged down with papers and be unproductive. If that starts to happen, I'll take a five-minute break and drink water and see if I need to write for a few minutes in my journal to get clarity. If I don't finish the project before noon, I'll schedule a follow-up session for Tuesday evening. When the two hours are up, I'll celebrate by meeting Anne at the park. She's the perfect person to do that with because she doesn't judge me. She'll let me brag about my efforts, and she'll be genuinely excited to hear about them.

Although writing a plan for a session can feel like a bothersome extra step, it can help you engage with this process in a fresh way that allows you to mindfully integrate a sacred approach.

You might not need a plan for every session. But a plan can be especially helpful when you're approaching an area or type of clutter that you've been avoiding or have felt defeated by in the past.

Possible Action

> Plan a clutter session addressing the following:

- ✧ What will your focus be?

- ✧ When will you work on it and for how long?

- ✧ How will you prepare and inspire yourself?

- ✧ To whom or what are you dedicating your session?

- ✧ What will you do to support your comfort?

- ✧ What are your hopes and fears as you anticipate the session?

- ✧ What will you do if you get stuck?

- ✧ What if you don't finish the project on time?

- ✧ What will you do after the session?

To find a printable worksheet for planning your clutter-clearing session, go to:

www.ClearingClutterAsASacredAct.com/

Build in Closure

Has something like the following ever happened to you?

You get all fired up to get rid of your clutter and start sorting stuff into piles. As time goes on you begin to feel weary and the decisions become more difficult. The sorted piles keep growing. The phone rings and you remember that you're late for an appointment. You rush around trying to get yourself out the door. When you come home a few hours later, the piles are there waiting for you. They're everywhere! Company is coming over, so you hastily gather up everything you've so carefully sorted and throw it into the spare bedroom.

Even if you haven't experienced this exact scenario, you've probably suffered through some version of it. Often, people find the energy to sort things into piles, but don't take the process any further. Either they live their lives around the piles, or the sorted stuff gets swept back into the blur of the rest of the clutter. It's an uninspiring cycle that can evoke hopelessness about ever making real change. You never get the satisfaction of finishing the project. You never feel done.

Here's an alternative: Build closure into every session.

Once you've planned what you're going to work on and for how long, you simply set a timer to go off halfway, or a third of the way through your allotted time. That first part of your session is your sorting time. Then, when the timer goes off, you shift gears and move to the closure step. Set the timer for the remaining time and start bringing your attention to each pile.

Here's how the closure step works:

Maybe one of your sorting categories is for things you intend to RELOCATE. Those are the items you'll keep but will move to another room or location. When the timer rings, you'll transition to the closure step and deliver the RELOCATE items to the spots where they belong. Toothbrushes will go back into the bathroom. Needle and thread will go into a box or basket with other sewing items. And so on.

Perhaps you have another category called GIVE AWAY. In this case, the closure step involves figuring out to whom or where you're going to donate the items, then getting them ready to go.

During closure, things that need to be filed can be filed. Things that need to be shredded can be shredded.

The closure step is often more challenging than the sorting step. That's because it gets into the details of what needs to happen next. It requires some realistic thinking. Sometimes you're forced to admit, *"I want to keep this but there's no real space for it."* Sometimes you won't know the answers to the questions that come up. *"Where in my town can I get rid of a used exercise bike that's slightly broken?"*

That's okay. Just do your best to move forward with whatever you can. Then make a list of the questions you have about the remaining objects and plan a time for researching answers.

Whether or not you figure out what to do with every single item, if you practice the closure step, you'll have more of a sense of completion at the end of each clutter session and more of a feeling of making progress with the larger process.

Possible Actions

> ➤ As you prepare for a clutter session, decide on your sorting categories. Use sticky notes to label stackable bins or boxes with titles like KEEP, GIVE AWAY, CAN'T DECIDE. Or get more elaborate and use labels like RELOCATE, NEEDS A SPACE, or ATTIC. Keep your sorting categories simple and do your best to make them relevant to your project and helpful to you.

➤ Set your timer for one half or one third of your allotted clutter session. Spend that time sorting. Then spend the remaining time following through on what you've sorted.

➤ If you have questions about where to donate or discard certain items, make a list of your questions, and put them in a section of your Clutter Notebook or whatever you're using as a Sacred Container for your process. Then, schedule a specific time dedicated to researching the answers to those questions.

➤ For ideas, prompts, and practices that can help with emotionally loaded items, read the next chapter, Create Your Emotional Box.

Create Your Emotional Box

When you're going through your stuff and making decisions about what to keep and what to release, it's likely you'll come across some emotionally loaded items.

It's not surprising that the love letters from the spouse who left you are likely to stir up big feelings. It's even somewhat understandable that it's a struggle to figure out what to do with the ceramic frog collection you used to love. But why in the world would that shampoo bottle under the bathroom sink bring tears to your eyes? Why are you feeling stuck and staring at a little plastic toy nobody wants or needs? Why can't you just quickly decide to get rid of that sweater full of holes?

When there aren't obvious reasons to explain your emotions, they can seem mystifying and even ridiculous. But emotions don't come from the world of logic. You may not be conscious of the associations and meanings certain objects and papers hold for you. That's why your clutter session can get so quickly derailed when you come upon an emotionally charged item. One moment you're efficiently deciding about one thing after another. The next you're swamped with feelings.

I take a gentle approach to clutter clearing. I don't encourage you to force a decision. I also don't recommend that you interrupt your sorting process to start unpacking big emotions. It's not a time to read those love letters or reminisce about good times you had while wearing that sweater. Just get whatever it is into a box labeled EMOTIONAL as quickly as possible. Then bring your attention back to sorting and making decisions about the items that are less emotionally fraught.

When you reach the closure step of your session, take another look at anything that ended up in your EMOTIONAL box. You may notice that you feel clearer about some of the items.

Refraining from making decisions before you're ready can give you room to relax and feel safe. That, in turn, can create space for you to do some inner sorting, while outwardly you continue to process other items.

When you come back to the things that previously felt too overwhelming, you might have more clarity. You might find yourself saying, *"Oh, I definitely want to keep that."* Or you may say, *"You know, I think I'd feel just fine about saying goodbye to that."*

Some objects might still feel too emotionally loaded for you to make decisions about. That's fine. Put those items back into the EMOTIONAL box and put a date on it. Then schedule a time in your calendar to revisit the box and its contents. Be sure that any emotional processing you do has its own time, separate from efficient sorting and practical information gathering.

Possible Actions

> ➤ Make a list of the kinds of items that would be likely to end up in your EMOTIONAL box. If any of them relate to or represent past chapters or endings in your life, make a note of that.

> ➤ Check out the writings in Chapter Seven of this book. They offer additional suggestions and writing prompts for processing emotionally loaded objects.

Keep Adjusting the Plan

Planning can be helpful. It greatly increases the possibility that you'll be able to make the changes you want to make.

But planning can also be scary. What if you don't do what you said you'd do? What if you get all invested in your plan, and then you disappoint yourself?

If you're afraid of your plan, it may be too rigid. Indeed, if it pressures you with overly ambitious or idealistic expectations and a sense that things must happen in a certain way, the plan itself can become a kind of clutter. Without the needed flexibility and breathing room, it can block you from going with the flow. It can increase your frustration and get in the way of spontaneous inspiration and unexpected possibilities. If this is how you're feeling about your plan, it may be time to revisit and readjust it.

For instance, you'll learn how to manage your relationship to time rather than having it manage you. Some people discover that they do best when they work ten minutes at a time. Working longer exhausts or overwhelms them or makes them feel resentful. Others do better if they can occasionally get a long stretch of hours to really dig in. Otherwise, they feel like they're having to shift gears too frequently. You can experiment with your sessions to determine the length of time that works for you. You'll also learn through practice how to know when it's time to stop.

As you try out the various writing processes and practices in this book, some will resonate and feel useful, and some won't. What's important is that you try some approaches you may not have thought of on your own, and that you check in regularly with your own inner wisdom and experience to determine what's proving to be most helpful to you.

Notice what uplifts and supports you, and what just feels like an added complication. Notice what gives you energy and what drains you. If something feels helpful, use it and make it your own. If it gets stale, reach for fresh inspiration from this book or other sources.

The point here is that you are in charge. I encourage you to keep showing up as best you can and trying what you're willing to try. You can choose to view every bit of your process—the victories, the struggles, and the readjustments—as sacred.

Possible Actions

➤ Write a list of what you already know works well for you when addressing your clutter. Write another list of approaches you know don't work for you.

➤ After doing a clutter session, or after trying any of the processes suggested in this book, write a little about how it went, what you'd like to try again, and any adjustments you want to make.

CHAPTER FIVE

Gentle Practices

The Art of Taking Breaks

I'm always encouraging people to take regular breaks when engaged in extended projects. As simple as that may sound, it's challenging.

Sometimes this is because people are hanging on to old beliefs like, *"Breaks are for wimps."* They may believe that mature, successful people keep their nose to the grindstone until the work is done. Not to do so would mean they were a slacker or a loser.

Some people who are highly distractible are suspicious of taking breaks. They're afraid—and possibly for good reason—that if they leave the project, they'll get sidetracked and never return to it.

Still, because of what I've seen in my work with many clients and with my own projects over the years, I persist in proclaiming that breaks are crucial to thoughtful, self-loving, and, ultimately, successful clutter clearing. Stopping to replenish your body, mind, and spirit helps you hang in there for the long-haul—staying engaged and making better decisions as you go. Personally, I notice, over and over, that even though I'm sometimes tempted to power through without stopping, everything goes better if I allow myself time to rest and restore.

There is an art to taking breaks well. If it doesn't come easily to you, here are some strategies to try.

- ✧ Establish regular "break alerts." Set a timer or alarm to go off every hour or two. Or ask a friend to call or stop by at a specific time for a check-in.

- ✧ Decide how long your breaks will be. Make them long enough to be refreshing, but short enough that they don't break your momentum. Five to thirty minutes is often about right.

- ✧ Leave a written clue to help you pick up where you left off. Leaving yourself a quick note that tells you what to do next when the break is over can save you wasted re-grouping time.

- ✧ Start breaks by asking, *"What do I need?"* Are you thirsty? Hungry? Needing to stretch? If you're coming up blank, try writing freely for a few minutes about how the project is going—what's working and what isn't.

✧ Build in transitions to help you return to work. You can set a timer. Many phone timers can be set to play a piece of music you find motivating. You might arrange for someone to guide you gently but firmly back to the task. You might encourage yourself back to your clutter clearing by saying phrases like, *"I'm going to feel so glad I did this,"* or *"Step by step, I'm getting this done,"* or *"I don't have to do this perfectly."*

✧ When the break is over, and you've returned to your project, start by reading the clue you left yourself. That will allow you to continue your momentum.

Possible Actions

➤ If you tend to resist breaks, list some of the beliefs you have about people who take breaks. Circle any of the beliefs you feel willing to challenge.

➤ As you anticipate doing a major decluttering session, spend five minutes writing a description of what your breaks will look like. Decide how often and how long your breaks will be and how you'll transition into and out of them. Then put your supports in place—set your timer, ask a friend to call you, give yourself verbal pats on the back—to help ensure that you follow the plan you set out.

Reframing Repetition

I like to think that repetition comes easily to me. In fact, it does—when the task is something engaging and pleasurable. It's a different story if the task requires regular effort at something difficult or boring. I remember how skillfully I avoided practicing my cello in the fourth grade. I spent most of the assigned 30-minute practice time unpacking my case, rosining the bow, and polishing and tuning my instrument.

You'd think that, as a clutter coach, I'd be a master at staying on top of repetitive housekeeping chores. Truthfully, they are an ongoing challenge for me, especially when I'd rather relax into my comfort zone or engage in grander adventures or creative activities.

Repetitive chores have a bad reputation. They are often the territory of unpaid or underpaid workers. They are associated with dreary servitude. Their results are often ignored, sometimes harshly judged, and rarely appreciated. It's no wonder many people avoid such chores or rebel against them.

It helps me to remember that repetition is an essential ingredient in our lives. The seasons repeat their sequence each year. Morning follows night. The repeating chorus in a song allows us to join in and be part of the singing. And there is power to repetition when we're practicing a skill, a scale, a language, or a new mindset. Repetition helps us build the foundation when we're trying to achieve new proficiency and open new possibilities.

There is also something beautiful about the humble, repetitive tasks that create the underlying rhythm of our lives. Without them, things fall apart: There are no clean clothes. There is nothing to eat. We can't find our keys.

Repetitive chores quietly support our functioning in a multitude of ways. They also provide some hidden benefits I find compelling:

⟡ They give my brain a rest. When life feels too complicated, and I've got decision-making fatigue, it can be soothing to chop some vegetables or put my hands into sudsy water and scrub a pile of dishes. It's a pleasure not to have to be smart for a while. I can invite my body to do something it already knows how to do. While I'm at it, I can have a relaxed conversation, listen to a podcast or audiobook, sing along with music, or enjoy some quiet time.

⟡ Repetitive tasks calm my anxieties. If I'm worried about something, the reassuring rhythm of a broom or rake can help move my energy and make productive use of it.

⟡ They reboot my creative process. When I'm working too hard at writing or making a piece of art, and I'm feeling stuck, repetitive chores give me permission to let go of the pressure to be original and interesting. My brain can shift gears. While I'm wiping off the counters, my project can simmer on the back burner of my consciousness. The simple task of putting dishes back into the cupboards often helps me gain some inner clarity. Afterwards, I'm ready to return to my project with fresh energy and inspiration.

✧ Repetitive tasks can be devotional gestures. Chores that must be done again and again, over and over, can be a way for me to physically engage with my home—tending it, blessing it, and expressing my gratitude. They fluff up the energy and make my living spaces more beautiful. My house feels loved, and I feel more at home there. As I tend my home, I tend my life.

There's no question that repetitive tasks can be a nuisance. They can be boring. No one should be stuck doing them all the time. But they are also important, potentially sacred acts.

Possible Actions

➢ Make a list of repetitive tasks you tend to avoid. Circle one to focus on.

➢ Write a description of yourself engaging in that task in a fresh way that helps to shift how you perceive it. Then try doing this task, keeping your new perception in mind.

Little Gestures

Do you ever find yourself making big pronouncements when you get fed up with your current reality? Sometimes it feels like we must change everything about our lives all at once. Unless it's a dramatic, all-encompassing gesture, it can seem like it doesn't count for much.

Grand pronouncements can be invigorating and motivating. But sometimes they are a set-up for disappointment. To the extent that they go uncompleted or unfulfilled, they can undermine your self-confidence. They can also affect other's trust in your word.

When people start making New Year's resolutions or declaring major changes, I think about my grandfather, Henry Eldridge Gentry. He was a skilled sign painter in Richmond, Virginia, back in the days when signs were carefully painted by hand. He was not one for grand pronouncements. He was a man of little gestures.

My mother described watching her father go through all the steps of making an especially fancy, hand-painted sign. He applied sheets of expensive gold leaf to its surface, gluing them down, then lightly brushed the excess into an envelope. Afterwards, he ran a comb through his hair, his bushy eyebrows, and his five o'clock shadow to make sure not a bit of gold dust was wasted.

According to my mother, he added to that envelope all year long. Then, each Christmas, he sold it and used the money it brought to buy a special gift for his family—something they could not otherwise afford. This was one of the many quiet actions that expressed who my grandfather was and what mattered to him.

It's the smaller gestures—the ones that occur behind the scenes, moment-to-moment, day-to-day—that build trust over time. This applies to relationships, work, projects, and your spiritual life. It also applies to your relationship with yourself.

It's one thing to grandly pronounce, *"I'm going to stop being a slob!"* It's another to notice the very moment you were about to throw your coat on the back of a chair, then to stop yourself and instead, hang your coat in the closet. You could promise sincerely, *"I'm going to be a more considerate housemate."* But a deeper, subtler shift comes when you realize you were about to leave a sink full of dishes for someone else to take care of, and, instead, you summon your own willingness to take care of them yourself.

It's a victory when you catch yourself about to repeat an old, unhelpful pattern, and you pause, shift gears, and practice a new, more intentional action. It's through these small changes that you create new pathways in your brain and actively increase your ability to put intentions into action.

When you say yes to something you'd normally say no to and you say no to something you'd habitually go along with, you strengthen your powers of choice and discernment. Whenever you start something you would normally postpone, or postpone something you'd tend to do impulsively, you create the space to remember your heart's desires and directly increase the possibility that they'll come true.

Possible Actions

> Make a list of five habits you'd like to change. Circle one you want to focus on.

> Imagine a new gesture you could put in place of that old habit.

> Imagine yourself about to engage in the old habit and shifting to your new gesture instead. Write about that experience as if it has already happened. Practice this new gesture as often as you can.

Embracing Spaciousness

I'm a believer in the power of spaciousness.

We try to solve problems and discomforts with more. More stuff. More gadgets. More opinions. More activity. But often what's needed is more space. Space to breathe. Space to think. Space around objects so they can be seen, found, used, and treasured.

Open space is valuable in so many ways. But it can also be unsettling. That's why, even as you consciously try to make more space in your home and schedule, you may end up filling them right back up again.

When I notice situations where I seem to be working against my own best intentions, I often get out my journal and write a letter to whatever is confusing me. Then I invite a letter back. It's amazing how often this leads to unexpectedly helpful information. You could write such a letter to spaciousness.

> *Dear Spaciousness,*
>
> *I think I want you in my life, but I must not. I try to free up my schedule, but then I start feeling anxious, lonely or scattered, or I start wasting time. Then I go back to saying yes to more commitments. My home is too full of stuff and I feel crowded and cramped. Plus, I'm always losing things. But when I imagine having a house that's spacious and sparse, I'm not sure I like it. It feels kind of lifeless. Empty. So, I make these big clutter-clearing plans, and then I avoid doing them. Spaciousness, is there any way I can bring you into my life that won't cause me to push you away again?*
>
> *Crowded and Confused*

It can be interesting to read the letter out loud and imagine that the recipient, spaciousness, is reading it. If you have the time and willingness, you can invite spaciousness to write a letter back to you. Just put your pen to paper and see what comes. Don't worry if it feels like you're just "making it up." Your imagination can be a helpful friend in this process. It's a kind of mindful pretending that can summon forth wisdom from a deeper part of yourself.

Dear Crowded and Confused,

I know I can be unsettling. It's because I hold the potential to change your life in big and little ways. When I'm around, anything can happen. That scares people sometimes. Maybe you just need to play with me in small amounts, so you can get used to me. I come in all sizes. So, for instance, just inviting a little of me into a drawer will allow you to open and close the drawer more easily. Adding a little more of me around your furniture will give you more room to move. If you insert me between the items on your to-do list, you can see what it feels like to go through your day in a more spacious way. I think you're going to love it. Since you can do these things in your own way and at your own pace, it doesn't have to be scary. As you get more comfortable with me, you'll probably find more ways to bring me into your life. Then the adventures can really begin. I'm looking forward to it.

Your friend-in-the-making,

Spaciousness

Possible Actions

> ➤ Take a moment to meditate on the word spaciousness. Notice the various thoughts and feelings that you associate with that word.

> ➤ Write a letter to spaciousness expressing your thoughts and feelings, hopes and fears. If you have any questions for spaciousness, feel free to ask them.

> ➤ Read the letter out loud. Then write a letter from spaciousness to you. Read that letter out loud. Write down anything that feels useful from the exchange of your letters.

Worry Clearing

Worries can be a kind of mental clutter. It's true they're sometimes useful. They can alert you to something that needs your attention. But many of us get stuck in a quagmire of endless worrying, constantly scanning the horizon for anything that could possibly go wrong.

Admittedly, being human is risky business, so it's not hard to find things to worry about. But being preoccupied with worries can keep you in a constantly fearful state. That just drains your energy, blocks your way, and fills up the spaces in your mind where fresh ideas could otherwise bloom.

If you notice that worries are constantly yammering at you, it's time to do some intentional worry-clearing.

OPTION 1: Turn toward the worries. Start by making a list of twelve things you're worried about. Then cross off any that are beyond your control. It's amazing how much time we can spend worrying about meteors that might hit or the messes other people are making of their lives. Crossing off your list the items you can't control isn't a sign that you don't care. It means that right now, when worries are overwhelming you, you're choosing to devote your time and energy to things you can do something about.

Once you've crossed off the worries related to things you can't control, your list should be made up of worries you do have the power to affect. Choose one. Then spend five minutes writing about it and any thoughts you have about how you could address it.

OPTION 2: Take a break to restore your perspective. Go outside: Stand in the rain. Inhale the scent of cedar trees. Look at a sky full of stars. Or go inside: Read a book of poetry. Make a sandwich. Hang out with someone who makes you laugh. Find your own ways to lighten the energy and re-inspire yourself.

OPTION 3: Engage in a doable, satisfying little project. Bring order to a sock drawer or a junk drawer. Glue something that was broken. Paint a wall a fresh color. The point here is to give yourself a project that allows you to experience transforming something through simple actions. Working with your hands and engaging with the physical world to make change can pull you out of your tangle of worries and move you into productive action. Remember that even modest projects can be devotional acts that you dedicate to someone or something you care about deeply.

Possible Action

> Choose one of the three suggested options and try it out. Note how you feel before you start and after you're finished.

When You're Not Feeling Well

I was sick recently. Even though it was just a cold, it hung on for weeks. It was tiring, messy, and inconvenient. I had work to do, home projects to complete, family obligations to fulfill, and a book to write.

After going through my usual pattern of denial, I finally had to admit that I felt lousy and wasn't getting any better. I cleared my work schedule, then immediately felt pressure to fill the open space with other projects. And—surprise here—as I went into those projects full steam ahead, my symptoms immediately got worse.

I was starting to make peace with the idea of slowing down and letting it all go for a while. Then I remembered a saying I'd heard some years ago:

> *Most of the brave and important acts in history have been performed by someone who wasn't feeling all that well that day.*

"See?" said a nagging inner voice. "Only wimps let a little sickness and discomfort stop them."

I often feel physical symptoms when I come up against an uncomfortable challenge. Many writers feel exhausted when they try to start writing. People who have big clutter-clearing plans sometimes feel sick to their stomachs when they try to begin. When aches, pains, and discomfort become the excuse to avoid the project, there's the chance we'll put it off forever. Facing challenges inevitably requires facing some discomfort.

But isn't it important to engage in self-care and compassion? Shouldn't we be listening to our bodies instead of overriding their messages to us? After all, sometimes one really does need to go to bed to heal.

What should you do if you have a challenge to face or things to accomplish, and your body is presenting symptoms? Do you surrender or push through? The answer can be complicated.

Faced with that question, I did what I usually do when I feel stuck. I pulled out my journal and posed some questions, answering with whatever words came out of my pen. I did this despite my own self-judgment that I was sounding awfully dramatic about a cold and a persistent cough. Here's some of what I wrote:

"What if I completely surrendered to this sickness?"

I would collapse. Give up. Assume I'll be sick forever. I would let being a "sick person" become my identity. I would never accomplish anything again. I wouldn't challenge myself in any way. I'd be apathetic and give up all hope.

"What if I denied this sickness?"

I would just pretend I was well. I would push myself to do everything on my list and keep all my appointments and keep up my regular rhythms. I wouldn't get enough rest. I'd likely get sicker and sicker. And I'd probably spread my sickness to other people.

Then I challenged myself to ask a question that would invite a third alternative.

"How can I face this sickness honestly, bravely, and creatively?"

I can view the challenge of getting well as the most important thing and a crucial step toward my other priorities. I can take the need for rest seriously. I can honestly name what I can and can't accomplish while still giving myself the care I need. I can say yes to slowly cleaning out the cupboard under the sink, being sure to allow myself to rest during the process. I can say no to pruning the bushes or painting the kitchen. Yes, to writing, but only a little at a time. Maybe I can establish a rhythm of resting, feeding my soul, taking care of my body, writing in small chunks, and doing a few quiet tasks that don't take much thought or energy but help me tend my life. I can remember the value of quiet. I can make space for the sacred. I can back off from my social life and my routines and get some perspective. This can be a time to slow down and integrate so I can make a fresh start.

Little injuries and bouts of sickness give us opportunities to practice working with the various limitations life inevitably presents. Discerning when to surrender, when to push through, and how to work creatively and realistically with what arises is an important life skill. It's also a crucial one for effectively clearing any kind of clutter.

Possible Actions

> ➤ List any physical issues that interfere with your clutter-clearing.

> ➤ Spend five minutes writing about what it would look like to navigate those limitations honestly, bravely, and creatively.

Celebrating Your Victories

Have you ever experienced this?

You've started making some real headway clearing clutter. But instead of appreciating your effort and progress, you just feel overwhelmed by the remaining clutter. All you can see is the prospect of endlessly slogging through one pile of stuff after another. Your energy fizzles.

This underscores why it's so important to periodically stop and savor what you've accomplished in this process. Skipping over this step can be a recipe for burying your momentum.

People may have taught you that it's self-centered and vain to boast or enjoy your victories. If you did excitedly share something you'd accomplished, maybe you were met with deflating responses. The person you told didn't care, didn't get it, or felt threatened to see you making progress.

Even if no one in your life discouraged you directly, you might have found your own ways to discount your progress. *"How dare I be excited about clearing some clutter when I live in a world with so many big problems and so many people in need?"*

But remember, clearing clutter is one of those seemingly insignificant endeavors that holds life-changing potential, even though the tasks it requires can feel trivial or boring. That's why you need all the help you can get to honor your efforts and sustain your momentum. One way to do that is to make your process meaningful in every way you can. Another way is to celebrate your victories, big and small.

It can be as simple as taking a photo of the space you've decluttered, giving yourself a gold star, doing a happy dance, or calling up a friend who will cheer you on. For the bigger victories, you might want to plan something more elaborate— an outing, a party, or some other treat that is special to you.

To help keep on track with your clutter-clearing plans—even when the process gets challenging—look for big and small ways to bask in the delight of your victories and accomplishments.

Possible Actions

➢ Make a section in your Sacred Container to write down your clutter-clearing, space-creating victories. Include photos.

➢ Make a list of ways to celebrate your big and little clutter-clearing victories.

CHAPTER SIX

Making Peace with Time

Your Relationship with Time

We are all in relationship with time. How we feel about it and interact with it affects every aspect of our lives.

How would you describe your relationship with time? What beliefs do you have about it? What feelings does it stir up to think about time?

It can be helpful to write a letter to time, expressing what you feel. Write whatever comes, then sign off in a way that feels right to you.

Dear Time,

I am so annoyed with you. Sometimes you chase me around and make me feel frantic. Other times, like when I'm visiting Jean in the hospital, you just drag so slowly. You never cooperate with me. When I'm driving to work, I swear you speed up and trick me into being late. And you're constantly taunting me about how life is short and I'd better get moving and do something important. It drives me crazy. I wish I could ignore you but that doesn't seem to be an option.

Fed Up

Read the letter you've written and notice the tone you've taken. It may or may not surprise you.

Then, if you're willing, invite time to write you a reply. Be open to whatever time has to say, even if it sounds strange. Allow the words to flow out of your pen or onto your screen freely and without judgment.

Dear Fed Up,

I'm so sorry you've been having such a miserable experience with me. But listen. This isn't working. You try to control me and then you ignore me. You get mad at me for existing. You get upset that things take time. You're forgetting that I'm a precious gift. It's up to you what you do with me. If you engage with me intentionally, I have great treasures to share. If you ignore me then, yes, I'll probably play tricks on you to get your attention. But I don't do it to be mean. I just want you to wake up and engage with me. Give me my due. Honor me. Make real decisions about what you're going to do with me. When you do, I'll meet you halfway. I may still speed up and slow down, but in ways that benefit you. First, though, we need to be in better communication. Thanks for opening the door to that. I'm looking forward to more.

Time

Possible Actions

> ➤ Write a letter to time. Then read it out loud, imagining that time is reading it.

> ➤ Write a letter from time to you. Read it out loud. Then write down your observations about anything interesting or useful that emerged from your exchange of letters.

Time Titles

Once you decide to clear your clutter, it can be very frustrating to discover that your living space can't be immediately transformed and tidy. As the process unfolds, you'll inevitably make messes along the way. Clearing clutter is a transition, and as such, it takes time. Even if you're using helpful strategies and making progress, it's easy to feel like you're not being productive enough. Any transition process can bring up similar feelings.

During a time of transition in my own life, I found that I was browbeating myself for not accomplishing enough. Then a phrase popped into my head that seemed to capture the essence of what I was going through—UNDER CONSTRUCTION. It was what I have come to call a "time title." It was a meaningful label that gave me more clarity about what my focus needed to be during that phase of my life.

Giving a title to the life chapter or transition process that you're currently navigating can help you see it as real and worthy of your time and attention. It validates saying yes to some things and no to others. It's also a reminder that this is just one chapter. There will be others with different titles.

When a time title occurs to you, it can be helpful to explore it further. I chose to use the letters of the words UNDER CONSTRUCTION to prompt the lines of a poem. I wrote quickly and didn't overthink. I let myself be surprised by the lines that emerged from each letter of the two-word phrase.

Using this time when I am
Not having to be so public, I am making
Decisions quietly and privately,
Entertaining possibilities and alternate
Realities.

Curiosity has a chance to blossom.
Outside of constrictions and expectations, with
None of the usual pressures to
Stay productive and understandable, this
Time is for me,
Restorative and
Ultimately fertile, as the
Climate within changes, and I can listen for right
Timing.
It is a relief and a joy and a gift
Only I can give myself.
No need to judge as I nudge this unfolding.

After I wrote the poem, I read it aloud, then wrote a few lines of reflection:

> *What a relief. This gives me permission to take the sorting time I need without seeing it as a weakness. I can wholeheartedly give myself this time to work behind the scenes.*

Time titles are also helpful for smaller chunks of time. For instance, when you plan a month, week, or day, you may want to include titles such as FAMILY TIME, TIME FOR ME, REST TIME, ERRAND TIME or time titles for whatever activities and focuses are priorities for you. It's a flexible way of planning. When that time arrives, you can decide what form your FAMILY TIME, REST TIME, or ERRAND TIME will take.

Possible Actions

➤ Think about some possible titles for the current chapter in your life story. Choose a title that fits.

➤ Write for five minutes starting with the words, *This chapter of my life is about...*

➤ If you were going to plan out the next week, what time titles would it be important to include?

Gertrude Time

You may long for order. You may fear getting buried in the mess. But you might also secretly worry that to clear your clutter is to stop being you. What if it means you're no longer creative, quirky and interesting, and instead you're becoming a fussy, boring drudge, obsessed with dust and tidiness?

Gertrude is a character from a book I wrote called *The Bear's Gift*. She's the essence of a practical hard worker. She loves making lists and crossing things off as she does them. It soothes her to put things away. She loves making order in a messy drawer, clearing surfaces, and getting things functioning.

I don't want to be Gertrude all the time, but I sometimes need her energy, willingness, and skills. So I practice taking what I call "Gertrude time."

For instance, if I've been immersed in a project and have been creating little pockets of chaos, I'll set a timer and for ten minutes, I'll become Gertrude. Like an actor stepping into a role, I'll embody Gertrude's focus and her satisfaction in taking care of business. I'll look through her eyes at the floor around me and start picking things up and putting them away. I'll even enjoy it. After all, it's just ten minutes. When the time's up, I'm free to express other aspects of myself.

It's amazing! At the end of my ten minutes of Gertrude time, my space looks surprisingly less cluttered. That's probably because I was fully committed and present in the activity. It turns out that a focused ten minutes can be way more productive than an unfocused hour. Because it was such a brief time commitment, I was able to jump in with both feet. My rebellious self—the one who doesn't want to be neat and tidy—did not sabotage me.

Gertrude time is also helpful for people who have limited time, unpredictable time, or limited energy. It counteracts the belief that if your time is restricted, you can't get anything done.

Gertrude Time allows you to introduce order in increments. It helps keep the chaos at bay. It also helps you build positive associations with Gertrude-like behaviors.

Possible Actions

> ➤ Make a list of possible names to assign to the energy you want to embody in your ten minutes of focused clean-up time. Pick one that works best for you. Feel free to use the name Gertrude if it appeals to you, but if you prefer a different name, use that instead.

> ➤ Is there a prop of some kind that would help you embody that focused, clean-up energy? Maybe you could put on an apron, some clean-up gloves, or a special hat. You might also choose music that helps you get in the mood. Jot down a few ideas about what props or other supports could help you get into character quickly.

> ➤ Choose an area that has gotten covered with things that need to be put away. Set a timer and spend ten minutes practicing Gertrude time. Then make a note about how it went for you.

Consulting Your Hat

Even when you're ready, willing, and have carved out the time for clutter clearing, it can be hard to know where to start. It might seem like all your unfinished projects and deferred tasks are simultaneously vying for your attention, and you're supposed to be addressing all of them at once. Since that's impossible, you might get caught up stressing about what's the most important thing to do first. All of this often leads to spinning your wheels instead of getting things done.

One option is to consult an organizing book. Many of them have prescriptions that tell you clearly what to do and what sequence to follow. Their approaches may or may not fit for you.

You could consult a friend or professional. Their opinion on the matter might be just what you need, or it might not feel quite right. In either case, this could be informative.

You might also consult your journal and ask the question, "*Where should I start?*" Writing for five minutes often brings some clarity.

I often find that it doesn't really matter what comes first. I just need to start somewhere, do one thing, and get some movement where I've been stuck. Then, if I still have time, energy, and focus, I can use that momentum to do something else on the list. At such times, my best option is usually to engage in a practice I call "consulting my hat."

Here's how it works. First, I make a list of twelve things I think I should be doing with the time I have. They could be projects that involve tending, fixing or cleaning, like replacing the furnace filter or gluing something that's been broken. They could be errands, like delivering clothes to the thrift store and cardboard boxes to the recycling center. They could be unfinished projects I haven't been able to revisit, like the half-sorted box of papers or the cupboard I only partially organized.

I have a set of numbers, 1 to 12, on pieces of colored cardstock one-inch square. I created them several years ago and just keep re-using them. Once I've made my list of twelve items, I put their corresponding numbers into a hat. Then I stir them around and pick one. Whatever I pick is the first thing to do. An alternative is to throw a pair of dice into the hat, shake them up, then dump them onto a table to see what number comes up.

I love this approach. It has a playful, yet sacred feel to it. I'm inviting the fates to guide me in my process and trusting that whatever number comes up, it will guide me where I need to go. It surprises me. It feels fluid. Often, after I do the first thing my hat suggests, my intuition engages and leads me to the next right thing to do. If not, I just draw another number out of the hat.

Since any of the items on your list would be helpful things to do, you don't have to be overly rigid about following this system. If you reach into the hat and pick something that brings up total dread or a feeling of rebelliousness, throw it back and pick something else. You'll still get something done and create some momentum. You can use this technique whether you have an hour, several hours, a whole day, or a weekend to devote to it.

I sometimes assign myself Hat Days—entire unstructured days when I allow the hat to be my guide. These days can be surprisingly enjoyable and satisfyingly productive. They give me permission to fully focus on one thing at a time, instead of a whole list all at once. What a relief! I love the way this gentle, organic structure gives shape to a shapeless day.

You can also mix some fun or relaxing things into your Hat Day. If you have a whole day, why not include some pleasurable and uplifting thirty-minute or hour-long activity that you don't often allow yourself?

You might call a friend you haven't talked to in a while, read a chapter in a novel, or go roller skating if that makes you happy.

Possible Actions

> ➢ Find a hat that you like but don't tend to wear. Dedicate it to the "consulting your hat" process. Then either create a set of numbers, 1-12, or find a pair of dice to keep in the hat.

> ➢ Make a list of no more than twelve items. It can include any combination of projects that involve repairing, fixing or cleaning; unfinished projects; and errands you've been putting off. You can also include pleasurable activities you haven't been allowing yourself. Then consult your hat next time you have a chunk of unstructured time and an intention to be productive.

Shifting Gears

The Greek words *chronos* and *kairos* have been particularly helpful to my thinking about the different ways we orient ourselves to time. Chronos refers to the chronological, sequential, measured time of clocks and calendars. Kairos refers to an experience of time that is deeply engaged in the moment.

Some people spend their lives constantly in chronos time, efficiently going from task to task and obligation to obligation. They're punctual. They're responsible. They're aware of time running out. But it can keep them from fully and passionately engaging with their lives.

Others spend much of their lives in kairos time. These people are often inspired and can experience rich engagement. But important aspects of their personal and professional lives can suffer from neglect. They're often late for appointments or forget them altogether.

It's helpful to strike a balance between those two orientations to time. It's also helpful to be able to gracefully shift from one to the other. When you're deeply engaged with a project, having to disengage and shift to something else can be a shock to the system. If you've been rushing through your day and striving to be efficient, it can be difficult to move out of that mode to spend quality time with loved ones.

Shifting from one mode to the other takes mental energy and awareness. So it helps if you plan and prepare for these transitions. For instance, it helps me to say, *"I'm going to give myself some kairos time this morning, but I'll need to shift to chronos time by 11."* I set a timer and sink fully into my kairos mindset, knowing that the timer will keep track and tell me when I need to start making the shift to chronos time.

If I have a meeting at 11, I don't set the timer for 11. Instead, I pad in extra time based on how long it will probably take me to disengage from my kairos task, leave myself a note about where I left off, prepare for my next activity, get myself out the door, drive there, and find the room where the meeting will take place.

The timer is just as useful when shifting from chronos to kairos time. If I've been involved with a busy schedule and time-sensitive commitments all day, I can set a timer to remind me when it's time to start the transition to kairos time. Sometimes it helps to set my phone alarm to play a song that will ease me into the energy that's right for the next activity.

Possible Actions

➢ Look at the activities you've planned for your day and notice when you're going to be in chronos time and when you're going to be in kairos time. Decide whether you need to build in more of either one. Think about what kinds of transitions you'll need to make and how you'll support yourself making them.

➢ Write down any other names you want to give to the different ways of experiencing time.

CHAPTER SEVEN

Letting Go

Let It Go

This can be sung to the tune of "Let It Snow," ©1945 Sammy Cahn and
Jule Styne.

We try to hang on forever
to each object and endeavor.
By now you would think we'd know
to let it go, let it go, let it go.

The trees drop their leaves in season.
They don't need to know the reason.
It just seems to help them grow
to let it go, let it go, let it go.

When we come face to face with change,
it's time to open our minds and our eyes,
to be willing to rearrange,
and also to say some goodbyes.

When we're hanging on so tightly,
it keeps us from feeling sprightly.
To bring on that healthy glow,
let it go, let it go, let it go.

Addressing Emotionally Loaded Objects

Even as you strive to be decisive and efficient during a clutter-clearing session, you're likely to come across items that stop you in your tracks. Sometimes it's because they require more research. Often, it's because they are linked to life events and choices that still feel incomplete or unsettled.

To stay on task and keep your process moving forward, it's helpful to have a plan for dealing with these items. For instance, you might have your EMOTIONAL box (see page 58) chosen, labeled, and ready to catch and hold the emotionally loaded objects and papers that might slow you down.

Many of the emotionally loaded items you encounter will be linked to losses and changes. You might come across clothing from when you were a different body size or find papers from the book you started to write but abandoned when your mother got ill.

Life is filled with shifts, endings, and readjustments. Whether a change is positive or negative, planned or unplanned, chosen, or foisted upon you, it may well be associated with a mix of emotions.

Major life transitions often bring a complex array of feelings. That's because transitions represent new beginnings, but also endings of certain roles and activities. For instance, even though weddings are usually happy occasions, they can also be stressful. They signal moving into a new chapter of one's life with new expectations and responsibilities. Similarly, the much-anticipated birth of a healthy, wanted child involves sacrifice and letting go of some personal freedom. And while the death of a loved one can be devastating, it can also be filled with unexpectedly beautiful moments.

As you've traveled through your various life changes, you may not have had time or the wherewithal to process and integrate all that was happening around you and within you. The inconvenient, unexpected, or unacknowledged emotions that you pushed aside back then might surface now as free-floating anger, vague sadness, or wariness. You may feel stuck, apathetic, or lost. Some part of you may still be asking a past, unresolved event, *"Hey! What happened?"* Resistance to life's changes and transitions can manifest in your living space as piles of related papers and artifacts.

Other emotionally loaded belongings may represent what has not happened in your life. When you start to dig in, you may come across props, materials, and supplies for a different life than the one you're currently living. There might be cooking equipment and recipes for the domestic person you feel you ought to be but aren't. There may be paints, brushes, and easels you've never given yourself time to use.

Belongings can hold all kinds of associations. That cello in the corner may represent a past victory or defeat, a dream unrealized, or someone else's expectations for you.

As you engage in your sorting process, you'll find that some emotionally charged items are fairly easy to deal with. You have clarity about whether to keep them or let them go. That can be an indicator that you've made some measure of peace with whatever chapter or choice the item represents.

The belongings that are more emotionally confusing will require a different kind of attention. That's why I encourage you not to let them derail your process, but to place them immediately into the EMOTIONAL box to address later. Don't worry if you don't understand why a hairbrush or a sweater full of holes brings tears to your eyes. Trust your emotional response and simply put them into the EMOTIONAL box.

The second part of your clutter-clearing session will be devoted to following up on the different categories you've sorted. This is when you'll deliver things to their proper homes, file what needs to be filed, and decide where you'll be donating things. You'll also take a second look at the items you've placed in your EMOTIONAL box. You may find that, having set them aside for a bit, it's now easier to decide what to do with them.

The emotional items you aren't ready to make decisions about can stay in the EMOTIONAL box for now. Put a date on the box. Note in your calendar when you'll take another look at its contents.

If any of the items that end up in your EMOTIONAL box are clearly related to a recent profound loss, you can group them together into one container or area. You may need additional time before you're ready to engage with and decide about those items.

For example, you might create a box and give it a title that is specifically related to a person or event, like MOM'S THINGS, or THE ACCIDENT. This will alert you to the emotional territory you'll be entering when you open the box later. Eventually, in whatever time it takes—one month, three months, a year—you may feel more able to address and make decisions about the things in that box.

It can take time to slow down and explore your thoughts and feelings about an emotionally charged object. But doing so can make your overall clutter-clearing process more efficient and effective. You don't have to process every single object. Engaging deeply with one item that represents an event, relationship, or transition can bring clarity about what to do with whole categories of things. I recommend scheduling separate time for the deeper emotional processing some objects might require.

The remaining chapters in this section of the book provide some approaches designed to help you explore and potentially release such objects and your emotions about them.

Possible Actions

> ➢ List some of the big life changes and adjustments you've gone through. Give them titles. Circle any you feel ready to explore. Avoid circling any that feel too upsetting.

> ➢ Choose one that you've circled and write for five minutes about any ways you may still be carrying physical or emotional baggage from that past chapter. As you write, try doing so with kindness and compassion toward yourself.

> ➢ Read your writing aloud, then write a sentence or two about any feelings that emerged while doing this exercise. You might want to linger with the feelings. Or you might do something to shift your mood. You can wash your face, take a walk, call someone, or listen to some happy music.

Telling the Stories

Our belongings hold stories for us. The box of your kids' school papers connects you to memories of the little children they once were. Grandmother's old dresser conjures her presence and the intricacies of the relationship you shared with her. Teaching materials passed on to you by your mentor remind you of how much she believed in you.

Emotionally loaded objects and papers have their own unique power. They hold our victories and our failures. They hold experiences of love and stories of times we were hurt, shamed or betrayed. Like artifacts in a museum, they hold the history of our lives.

When you're considering whether to keep or release an item in your EMOTIONAL box, it can be helpful to ask yourself how the object came into your life, what it represents for you, and what hopes and fears you've attached to it.

Telling the story of the item and exploring what it means to you can allow you to feel and express emotions it holds that got pushed aside or buried. What was unnamed can be named. What was stuck can move. Engaging in this kind of exploration while focusing on a watch, a pair of boots, or a set of dishes, can often clarify what to do with them next.

Once you write down the story of a piece of furniture or other emotionally charged item, it may become easier to give it away.

For instance, consider the dresser that holds precious memories of your grandmother but doesn't fit in your house. It's taking up space and making your life harder instead of easier. Luckily, you have a niece who needs a dresser. If she wants this one, you can pass it on to her along with the story of your relationship with your grandmother. If not, you can still share the story, then look for another home for the dresser.

If the item is broken, used up, or of no use or interest to anyone else, it may still have meaning for you. That matters. When you write the story of a broken lamp, you can take a photo of it, put it in the Goodbye section of your Sacred Container (see page 13), then give the lamp away or discard it. This gives you a way to honor part of your own story even as you let the object go. It also frees you from having to be the lamp's caretaker for the rest of your life. You've reclaimed the essence of what it was holding for you. Now you can release it more lightly.

Emotionally loaded objects can also be springboards for your creativity, whatever form that takes—poetry, songwriting painting, dance, quilt-making. Even the most humble, ordinary, inexpensive items can be charged with meaning because of their context. Giving full expression to their stories and allowing them to inspire other forms of art, can allow you to savor them, learn from them, and share them with others.

Possible Actions

> ➤ Choose an object that feels emotionally charged but not overwhelmingly distressing. Using the questions below as a guide, do a ten-minute writing exploring the object's story.
>
>> ✧ How did it come into my life?
>>
>> ✧ What chapter of my life does it represent?
>>
>> ✧ What hopes and fears have I attached to it?
>>
>> ✧ What meanings does it carry for me?
>
> ➤ Read aloud what you've written. Then write a couple of sentences about anything that strikes you as interesting or helpful. Notice whether you feel any clearer about what should happen next with the object.
>
> ➤ Consider the possibility that the object could inspire a creative work. Is there a poem, story, piece of art, or other form of creative expression it inspires? If so, note it in a section of your Sacred Container.

Talking to an Object

In other chapters, you've been invited to write letters to your clutter, your home, spaciousness, and time. It's a way of acknowledging that we're in relationship with all these things. Whether those relationships are close or distant, friendly or embattled, opening the lines of communication with them helps. In this chapter, I'll be suggesting ways to talk with your emotionally loaded objects.

I don't necessarily mean that you're speaking to the spirit of the object—that may or may not be how you experience it. But even if you're just "making it up," imagining what the hatbox or hammer would say to you can give you new ways to think about the item. Instead of dismissing your feelings as ridiculous or trying to force a quick decision, you are creating a fresh way to invite your inner guidance to make itself known and help you with this process.

> *Dear Hatbox,*
>
> *I think you are so beautiful. You come from an elegant era, and you remind me of my New York City aunts. I love your colors. You are such a satisfying shape. But you are one of so many boxes that I seem to hang onto. Why can't I let you go? I don't even wear hats.*
>
> *Your Ambivalent Admirer*

When the hatbox writes back, it may have some surprising suggestions.

> *You're right. I am exceptionally beautiful. I'm probably your very favorite box. I'm a treasure for you. A piece of art. An inspiration. If you give yourself full permission to keep me, you'll be able to loosen your grip on some of those boxes that aren't as beautiful or unique. Just know you're keeping the best of the best. And it's okay if you don't keep a hat in me. What if you gave me a real place in your home where people could see me? What if you displayed me proudly as a work of art? I am a holder of your dream of being a designer. Maybe I could be the place where you put little notes about your artistic ideas.*

A letter is one way to talk with objects. A dialogue can be an interesting and effective alternative because it allows for more give and take. Choose an object to talk to—a guitar, a vase, a box of toys, or any other object you feel is ripe for engaging with. You can record yourself speaking the two parts out loud and then listen to what unfolded. Or you can write the dialogue out like a script.

Me: Hello stuffed tiger. Are you willing to talk with me?

Tiger: Sure. Why not.

Me: Why are you still in my life?

Tiger: Well, what do you think about when you look at me?

Me: I think about when Bobbie was little. I also think about when our dachshund Gus chewed on you. I think about how I never thought time would go so fast.

Tiger: Do you think that by hanging on to me you can keep Bobbie from growing up and Gus from dying?

Me: Well, maybe. I guess that doesn't really make any sense since those things have already happened.

Tiger: It's okay. Emotions aren't logical. But I think it is time for me to go. I'm satisfied I did a good job of comforting Bobbie. Now I want to help you open some space in your life by saying a loving goodbye.

Possible Actions

> ➤ Spend five minutes writing a letter to an object you're curious about. Read it over and invite a letter back. Make a note of any fresh insights that emerge.

> ➤ Try having a conversation with an object. Do it out loud and record it or write it down like a script. Then, note any clarity that comes to you.

Honoring the Departed

Death is a universally challenging reality for human beings to grapple with. We do what we can to make peace with our own mortality and look for ways to feel connected with those we've lost.

Nonetheless, when someone close to you dies or disappears from your life, it can rock your very foundation. At such times, you might find yourself seeking ways to feel their love any way you can. You might find comfort in touching and holding objects they have left behind.

For example, after my mother's death, I found it comforting to go through her closets, read her writings, and look at her photographs. Her things held her history and helped me feel like she hadn't disappeared. The process of interacting with her belongings informed and deepened my sense of who she was as a person, beyond being my mother. When I put on her bathrobe, I felt like she was holding me and helping me through the ordeal of losing her. All her things seemed precious.

At first, because there may be so many objects associated with your loved one, it can be hard to know what to keep and what to let go. But going through their belongings when you're ready and making those choices is part of the goodbye ritual that may help you find some measure of peace. It can also prevent you from having a house crowded with their things. You and any other members of your household need room for your own tastes and preferences. You need room to grow your own lives.

That might require you to be discerning about what items left behind by loved ones get integrated into your home.

Because determining what to keep and what to release is a potent ritual, it's helpful if you can wait until you're emotionally ready for it. And once you are ready, the process of making decisions about these items will likely happen in stages. You do the first wave. You take a break. Then you see what you're ready to do next. The timing required for this process is different for everyone. While items are waiting to be processed, it's helpful to store them in a way that doesn't take over the main living spaces of your home.

Sometimes people don't get around to sorting through such objects at all because they feel that if they let something go, they're throwing the person away. If you have those concerns, remember that your loved one has passed on various things they cherished, inherited, and accumulated—deliberately or unintentionally. Some or all of that has come to you. Now you get to decide which of these things fit into your life and are a treasure for you and your descendants to keep. No matter how many items you keep or release, you can wrap the whole process of discernment in blessings and love.

In my process of going through my mother's things, I found that, over time, it became easier for me to identify the items that were treasures to me. As I clearly chose to keep those things, it became easier to release others.

Even if you lost someone a long time ago and feel you've waited way too long to go through this process, it's possible that now is exactly the right time.

> *"The best time to plant a tree is twenty years ago. The second-best time is now." – African Proverb*

As you determine that some objects need to be sold, donated, recycled, or even put in the trash, it can be helpful to say some words of goodbye and thanks. It's an opportunity to express your appreciation and love.

If the person was cruel or controlling, you may want to do a burning, burying, or shredding ritual with certain items, expressing your anger and sadness. If it feels right, you can also say words of forgiveness and wishes for healing. That's up to you.

If you come across things that are still too emotionally loaded to decide about, you can return to them after more time has passed. When you give yourself the time you need, doing what you can at each stage, you honor your unique grief process and pacing.

It can also be deeply helpful to spend time creating a scrapbook, piece of art, slideshow, shadowbox, shrine, quilt, song, or story that gathers your memories and impressions of the person. What you create can be simple or elaborate, funny or serious. It can express the best of who the person was or the complex mix of who you knew them to be. Whatever you choose to do, remember you don't need to do it perfectly. The point of this ritual of creating is to spend time with their essence and savor the gifts they gave you.

When you have the support and wherewithal to do it, this process can be meaningful and freeing. Clearing the clutter, claiming the treasures, wrapping the process in blessings, releasing some of the objects in meaningful ways, and creatively gathering the essence of your loved one, are all ways to honor their life and to give yourself permission to more fully claim and move forward with yours.

Possible Actions

> ➢ If you have lost someone, write for five minutes about where you are in the process of addressing their belongings. Take some time to describe your feelings.

> ➢ Describe what you feel is the next step in your process of honoring your loved one.

A Goodbye Ritual

We're used to having rituals when a person dies—a funeral or memorial service. We may have a burial or a scattering of ashes to honor who that person was and what they meant to us. It helps us say goodbye and bless them on their way. It allows us to more fully acknowledge that something has shifted. It helps us begin to catch up to the reality that life won't be the same.

Goodbye rituals can also be conducted for emotionally loaded belongings.

A woman I knew had a beautiful stone sculpture she adored. One day her husband accidentally backed into it with the car, causing irreparable damage. Every time she looked at the sculpture's broken remains, she felt furious at her husband.

After some time had passed, she decided that she needed to perform some sort of ritual to acknowledge the importance of this loss and to find a way to forgive her husband.

She made a ritual of first pulverizing the sculpture with a sledgehammer. This helped her express and release her anger. Then she scattered the little bits of stone onto her garden, saying words of blessing for her marriage. The ritual was rather simple, but it brought her some peace and helped her remember what she loved about her husband and their life together.

For years my father made tall, colorful, whimsical sculptures out of inexpensive materials. It was his way of releasing the stresses of his work. Over time, he created more sculptures than our house could comfortably hold.

One day I found him in the process of hacking one of them apart to throw in the garbage. I suggested that instead of destroying them and throwing them away, we figure out a ritual for releasing them. We brainstormed and together came up with the idea of having an "adopt-an-object" party. It was festive and fun and many of the objects found happy new homes. We took pictures of the party. He still takes great delight in seeing the photos of people carting their treasures away.

I had a huge collection of journals that I was lugging around in boxes. They were precious to me. They also felt like a burden. And I felt vulnerable about parts that I would not want anyone else to read.

I didn't know what to do. So I started my process of inquiry by writing a poem that expressed my mixed feelings.

My Journals

I have been keeping journals for twenty-four years—
ninety-three of them, spiral-bound
sketchbooks with no lines.

I open one up and there is my twenty-one-year-old self, naming
her truth, finding her voice.
I open another and my thirty-nine-year-old self is writing poetry
about chaos and order.

I want to preserve them—
to line them up chronologically in a wooden cabinet with glass
doors and a golden key.

I turn the page and remember now
that these are unedited journals.
Filling the space between strokes of brilliance are pages of dull
drivel, fatigue, envy,
a thousand recipes for self-improvement,
and infinite incriminating items I would hate
for my loved ones to discover.

Rotting and unsightly, this is the fertilizer for my life,
my relationships, my creations.
I want to put my journals in the compost pile,
bury them deep,
and invite the worms to have their fill.

These spiral sketchbooks hold all of me—
the writer who wants to mine them for gems,
the lazy one who can't be bothered,
the old woman who wants to look back,
the embarrassed one who wants to forget.

Now they sit in cardboard boxes in an old wooden garage,
surrounded by things we don't know how to keep and
don't know how to let go.

I worry that they are decomposing,
even as I wait, impatiently, for them to
turn back into soil.

After giving it some time, I felt sure that I wanted to release my journals. Ideally, I would have read every page, torn out everything I wanted to keep, and then burned the rest in an enormous bonfire. But I didn't want to spend the time it would have required for me to read them all. I also didn't have a place to safely and legally have a fire large enough. Instead, I came up with a simpler process that worked for me.

I randomly tore one page from each journal. I took those pages to a beach where I built a small fire. I read each one, then burned them, saying goodbye to them with love and appreciation. The parts of my journal that remained I thanked, blessed, and then had professionally shredded. I felt sad but relieved. Lighter.

After the ritual, I took a break from writing in journals. Then a fresh chapter opened. I took a class in journal therapy and started training at the Therapeutic Writing Institute. Eventually, I got certified as a journal therapist. Journal writing was back in my life in a new and vibrant way that I was able to weave into my work.

When you bring sacred intention to the releasing of emotionally loaded objects, the best of what they carried often finds fresh expression in your life.

Possible Actions

> ➢ Make a list of objects that might require a goodbye ritual. Circle one to work with.

> ➢ Write for five minutes about a possible ritual. Consider the following questions:

>> ✧ What chapter of my life is this object linked to?

>> ✧ What actions should be part of the ritual? Burying? Burning? Breaking? Giving? Telling?

>> ✧ Where should the ritual take place and who should be there?

>> ✧ What props are required?

>> ✧ What intention do I want to set for the ritual?

When Closure Feels Wrong

Just in case you are bound in place
by the belief that to move forward
is to abandon and betray all that came before,

listen.

After you've turned towards the past and said
thank you and goodbye,
spoken what words of forgiveness you could honestly say,
asked for absolution,
released what was dead weight,
and placed the true treasures into your pack,

you can turn,
and take a step in a fresh direction.

When you do,
my dear one, I promise
all the love that came before will be
in you and with you
every step of the way.

CHAPTER 8

Soul Spaces

What Is a Soul Space?

We don't just have relationships with people, belongings, and time. We also have relationships with spaces. Soul Spaces are the special places where you can be yourself, feel at home, and discover more about what you resonate with and love. They hold clues to who you've been and who you are becoming.

Although different places call to us at different times in our lives, there can also be threads of connection—certain qualities of space that consistently bring delight and inspiration, safety and comfort.

As you work on clearing physical clutter, you are making room for what matters. You are also working on making yourself more at home in your living space and your life. It's a good time to think about the Soul Spaces you've found, created, experienced, fantasized, and envisioned.

Childhood Soul Spaces

When you were a child, did you find or create special spaces or places that were just for you? Did you make a home for yourself under tables or in hidden corners where you could be alone? Did you create blanket forts, or did you secretly read under your covers with a flashlight? Did you find special trees or caves? Did you build treehouses or driftwood shelters on the beach?

Maybe you had rules about who could come in and who couldn't. Maybe you brought in special objects and arranged them just so. Maybe it was a place no one else knew about where you could be yourself, away from the opinions of others.

Your family's home may have been a Soul Space for you. If you moved around a lot as a child, there may have been one house, yard, or room that fit you exactly—one you missed and yearned for after leaving it.

What were your Soul Spaces when you were a child?

Possible Actions

> ➤ Make a list of the Soul Spaces you found or created as a child. It's fine to give them titles only you would understand. Think about the spaces that gave you permission to be your true self. Be sure to list only the ones that have positive associations. If no Childhood Soul Spaces come to mind, think about Soul Spaces you imagined or explored in your dreams, read about, or saw in movies.

> ➤ Look at your list of Childhood Soul Spaces. Circle one that you'd like to explore further. Spend at least five minutes writing what you remember about the space, including where it was, what was in it, what you did there, and what it felt like to be there. Read it aloud. Then write down the qualities of the space that seemed to be most important to you. You may want to share your writing with someone you love and ask them about their Childhood Soul Spaces.

> ➤ Do a drawing or collage of one of your Childhood Soul Spaces. Ask if it has any messages for you about your current environment. Write down anything it has to say.

Adulthood Soul Spaces

Adults have Soul Spaces, too. As you think back on your early adulthood, remember the different places you've lived. Are there any that you loved deeply? What was it like when you first started living by yourself, with a partner, or with a group of friends? Did you connect much to your environment? Were there rooms or homes that you felt expressed who you were and supported you in growing into yourself?

If you found it hard to create spaces that felt good to you, think about the homes and spaces of other people that spoke to your soul. What were the qualities that helped you feel at home? How did that change over the years?

If you have found it difficult to connect to indoor spaces, think about the outdoor spaces and landscapes that have lifted your spirits and comforted you.

Possible Actions

> ➢ As you reflect on the various spaces you've lived in and visited as an adult, make a list of rooms, homes, and landscapes that you felt a soulful connection to. This can also include current Soul Spaces.

> ➢ Choose one Adult Soul Space to write about in more detail. Take about five minutes. Then read it aloud and write a sentence or two about anything you notice.

> ➢ Draw or make a collage of one of your Adulthood Soul Spaces. Then notice whether it has any messages for you about your current environment.

Emerging Soul Spaces

What kinds of spaces are you most drawn to now? I encourage you to seek out spaces where you feel the most connection to your deepest self. Find places where you can hear yourself think and special spots that make your soul sing.

I wanted to build and deepen Gentle Approach Coaching—my practice dedicated to coaching people in clearing clutter and navigating transitions. I noticed that, these days, I feel most inspired and spiritually connected when I'm walking under trees. So I decided to dedicate my professional transition process to a cedar tree that stands in a forest of cedars about a fifteen-minute walk from my house.

You might wonder why I chose a tree for my dedication. How could a tree connect with or care about my coaching practice? I have no idea. But the ritual of visiting the tree and communing with its deep roots, solid trunk, and high-reaching branches seemed to help me hold steady with my vision.

Each time I visited the tree, I brought a flower or a coin as an offering and made a circle of branches around its trunk. Often, I'd come back to it and find the circle scattered, so I'd make a ritual of putting it right. It was a way of tending my dream.

One day when I visited my tree, I came across a little troop of girls from a nearby pre-school. Turns out they'd been regularly visiting and tending my tree, too. They were also building fairy houses around it and the surrounding trees. My Soul Space became even more sacred and powerful with this discovery.

Possible Actions

> ➤ Write about the kind of Soul Space that would support you in moving into the next chapter of your life.

> ➤ Or make a drawing or collage that expresses the qualities and particulars of your Emerging Soul Space.

CHAPTER NINE

Setting Intentions

Someday We'll Be Uncluttered

This can be sung to the tune of "Over the Rainbow," ©1939 Harold Arlen and Yip Harburg.

Someday we'll be uncluttered
and we'll find
endless love for ourselves
and absolute peace of mind.

Someday we will make choices
wise and true
doing only the things we're sure
we are meant to do.

Someday we'll let these fears go by
and leave our disappointments far behind us.
Where stacks of paper aren't so high
and our "to do's" don't make us sigh—
that's where you'll find us.

Someday we'll be uncluttered
but for now
we'll find love for each other
and for ourselves somehow.

'Though we're imperfect as can be,
compassion waits for you and me
right now.

A Dedicated Space

Here's a question that can be very useful—and even exciting to consider—when you're engaging in a clutter-clearing process: What are you making space for?

As you sort through your belongings, deciding what to keep and what to let go of, the clutter itself might offer clues about the new space you're creating. Some of the things you've hung onto are holding dreams that have not yet been realized. A book, map, or guitar might remind you of a past endeavor you abandoned or an adventure you never really began. While many of those dreams may no longer be relevant or resonant, some might still be deeply compelling.

If there is a project or activity calling to you—something you want to intentionally bring into your life—ask yourself if it requires a physical space.

When I decided I wanted to bring writing more fully into my life, I made a ritual of setting up a dedicated writing space. It was simple, with just a wooden table, a cup for pens, and a bouquet of flowers. I placed my journal and a few simple art supplies on a shelf within easy reach. I added a lamp to illuminate the space. Then I wrote a blessing for it.

It's a powerful ritual to create a dedicated space. There can also be power in the ritual of tending such a space.

When the time came to write this book, I knew I had plenty of things to say. But I was having trouble getting started. I was pressuring myself, and the words just weren't coming. It was time to slow down, get off the productivity track, and engage in an act of devotion. It was time to tend my writing space.

I polished my wooden table. I picked a fresh bouquet of flowers. I removed the dwindling pens from my cup and replaced them with fresh, colorful, smooth-flowing pens. I decorated a new journal and then wrote in it, dedicating it to my book project.

Then I looked up and noticed that the old bracket holding up the curtain rod above me was broken and wobbly. Repairing this was a chore I'd been avoiding. It involved dismantling, measuring, drilling a new hole, and screwing in a screw. It seemed like it should be simple, but I knew such chores often take longer than I think they will. I almost talked myself out of dealing with it.

Instead, I decided to treat the task as an act of devotion. That made all the difference. I didn't rush. I moved slowly and methodically. When I measured wrong and had to drill a new hole, I didn't berate myself. I just viewed each part of the endeavor as an expression of my commitment to this book. It was unexpectedly satisfying.

Creating a dedicated writing space was my way of inviting writing more fully into my life. Tending that space as an act of devotion reconnected me with the spirit of my book project. The words began to flow.

Possible Action

> ➤ Make a list of activities or projects you feel strongly compelled to bring more fully into your life. Put a check next to the ones that require a physical space or props. Circle the activity or project that calls to you most.

> ➤ When you feel ready, make a ritual of creating the space for this activity or project.

For a printable worksheet that can help you plan a dedicated space, go to:

www.ClearingClutterAsASacredAct.com/

Time Travel

Imagine that you carry within you every age you have ever been and every age you'll ever be. Through writing and other processes, you can access those younger and future versions of yourself to bestow compassion and forgiveness, gain understanding, and receive wise guidance.

Imagine how much it would have meant to you, during a difficult phase of your life, to have received a reassuring letter from your future self. You are that future self. You could write that letter with authority as you describe to your younger self how she survived and navigated those challenges. You could also let her know about some of the unexpectedly good things she has to look forward to.

Similarly, there is also a future version of yourself who can give you encouragement and reassurance. The processes and actions described below can help you access that future self to get a sense of your home and life a year from now.

Summoning Your Future Self

◊ Use your breath to quiet your mind and tune into a relaxed state.

◊ Imagine it is now one year from today.

◊ Look around at this future version of your life. What has changed and what has stayed the same over the year?

◊ What new spaces have you created?

◊ What new rhythms have become part of your life?

◊ How have you have been able to clear some significant pieces of clutter from your home, head, heart, and schedule?

◊ How does it feel to breathe and to move through this future space?

◊ As your future self, remember the experience of reading this book. What ideas and suggestions spoke to you and inspired you?

◊   Remember how you tried out some ideas, then adjusted them, making them your own.

◊   Remember the process you went through in the course of the year. Notice the obstacles you encountered. How did you overcome them?

◊   Notice that, although you traveled through your process imperfectly, some things that used to seem impossible now feel entirely possible.

Possible Actions

➤   Write a letter from your future self to your current self. Let your future self—the one you'll be one year from now—describe how your life looks and feels since you put some of the suggestions in this book into practice. Invite your future self to describe to your current self what helped the most in your process of change.

➤   After you've written the letter, read it aloud. Write down anything that strikes you as important or useful. You may also wish to write about how it felt to visit your future reality.

For a recorded entrance meditation to guide you through this process, visit:

www.ClearingClutterAsASacredAct.com/

Some Tips for Packing Light

Here I am with my overstuffed bags,
Packing cubes and luggage tags.
I have a feeling, but I'm just not sure
I have everything I need, plus a whole lot more.

Should I pack heavy? Or should I pack light?
I really don't know what's wrong or right.
I want to live adventurously
but I seem to want to bring my whole house with me.

It's so challenging to know what to take with you and what to leave behind as you head into any adventure—whether it's a trip or the next unfolding chapter of your life.

Fearing you won't have enough, you may tend to pack too much. But as you try to weed things out, you might worry that you'll go too far and not have what you need when you need it.

You may have been drawn to this book because you're trying to sort out what in your life is too much and what is not enough. Perhaps you have too much stuff and not enough space for it. Too many obligations and not enough time. Too many distractions and not enough focus on the things you care about most.

You may be trying to figure out what "enough" looks and feels like. What does it mean to have enough and be enough?

Does having enough ask that you have the props on hand for any endeavor you might choose to engage in? Does it require that you have available anything that anyone else might need? Does it assume that you will be the keeper of the family history and all its artifacts? Does it require you to be able to supply the missing part to whatever is broken or lacking?

What if past expectations and their accompanying props have become too much? What if an old role or identity has become clutter for you, and you decide to let it go?

Will you still be enough?

As you try to make sense of this, you might study books for organizing your home and your life. You might ask people you know for their opinions about what's the right amount of stuff in your home or the correct number of commitments in your schedule.

But ultimately, what matters is how it all feels to you and to those you share space with. Is it working? Do you have what you need for the life you want to be living now? Can you move forward without being overly encumbered by excess baggage?

Preparing for an actual trip can be an apt metaphor for this process. When I'm packing for a vacation, I do my best to bring what I'll need and to get it all to fit gracefully into my luggage. I usually pack and unpack several times trying to get it right. I often head out with a bag that feels overly full, even as I carry some lingering concerns that I still might not have exactly what I need.

Once I've settled into the trip, I often discover that I've packed imperfectly. But ultimately that doesn't really matter. I can make it work.

Now that I'm in my seventh decade, the phrase *packing light* has taken on new meaning. I've learned that there is no one right amount of stuff. Travels and life are filled with twists and turns, things you can plan for, and things you couldn't possibly predict. What each person needs to have with them at any given moment varies tremendously.

But I have developed an essential packing list of things that work very well for me, wherever I go.

These are the things I try never to leave home without:

✧ Flexibility and creative resourcefulness.

✧ A sense of humor.

✧ An open heart and mind.

✧ A willingness to play the fool and take reasonable risks.

✧ Some helpful rhythms of checking in with my inner wisdom, divine guidance, and common sense.

✧ A mix of humility and self-respect.

✧ An openness to perceiving all aspects of my imperfect life as sacred.

If I have these things on hand, I'm packing light, no matter where I'm going and regardless of what I've weeded out or held onto.

Possible Actions

➢ Write for five minutes exploring what it means to have or to be "enough." What would it look and feel like if you had enough belongings, supplies, and activities, as well as enough spaciousness in your home and schedule?

➢ Write for five minutes about what it would mean to pack light for the phase of your life you're heading into.

➢ Read both of your writings aloud. Then write a few sentences reflecting on your writings. What feels helpful? What interests you?

Closing Words

Congratulations! You have arrived at the end of *Clearing Clutter as a Sacred Act*!

You may have gotten here by picking the book up as the spirit moved you, opening it at random for inspiration and guidance. If so, take a moment to reflect and ask yourself whether what you found was helpful. If it was, you might want to continue with that approach. Or you might feel more drawn to reading the whole book as a progression of ideas and practices.

If you've read the book from start to finish, I invite you to stop and take a short pause before moving on. Let the fact that you've completed it sink in. Reflect on or write about ideas or suggestions that were useful or caught your attention or interest.

If you've taken the time and energy to fully engage with the book, doing writings and trying out practices, bravo! That takes courage and fortitude. Now give yourself time to breathe, look back on what you've done, and celebrate what you've accomplished! After you've taken a break, you can decide whether you've done enough for now or you've created some momentum you want to continue.

Regardless of how you've arrived at these closing words, there is no expectation that you should have your clutter situation perfectly addressed. One of the most fundamental principles of this book is that clutter clearing is an unfolding process. The book is designed so you can return to it again and again as you need and want to. Even practices and prompts you've done before are likely to hold different meanings as you and your circumstances change. Different parts of the book will call to you in different ways at different times.

Your process will always have its own shape and pacing. I hope that each time you return to *Clearing Clutter as a Sacred Act,* you'll give yourself full permission to take what you need and let the rest go.

Many blessings for your process, whatever shape it takes. May it be a sacred one.

Helpful Resources

This book's companion website includes worksheets, recorded entrance meditations for writing processes, and other resources designed to support your clutter-clearing process with gentleness, imagination, and sacred intention. To access those resources, go to:

www.ClearingClutterAsASacredAct.com/

You can also access the resource page by scanning the code below with a smartphone:

About the Author

Carolyn Koehnline lives in Bellingham, Washington, where she is an author, artist, psychotherapist, personal coach, and certified journal therapist. She is known for her compassionate approach to clearing physical, mental, emotional, and schedule clutter to make room for what matters.

Carolyn is also the creator of Gentle Approach Coaching, a  flexible method that utilizes a supportive approach, accessible tools, and simple practices to ease transitions and facilitate change. A lifelong journal keeper and a faculty member of the Therapeutic Writing Institute (https://twinstitute.net), Carolyn incorporates writing processes into much of what she does.

Carolyn can be contacted through her website:
www.GentleApproachCoaching.com

Other Books by Carolyn Koehnline

Carolyn has published two other books: *Confronting Your Clutter* and *The Bear's Gift*, a transformational tale for all ages, which she also illustrated. They are available at:

www.GentleApproachCoaching.com

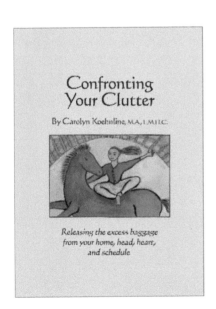